"Maya Feller takes us around the world to discover the healthy techniques and ingredients from an incredible range of countries. **A treasure trove of new ideas beyond the same old 'healthy' recipes,** this book will introduce you to new cuisines—and teach you how to recreate your favorite flavors in your home kitchen!"

—Jason Wachob, founder and co-CEO of MindBodyGreen

"In this beautiful cookbook, **Maya reclaims the healthy foods that nourished diverse people for generations** and shows everyone the way to a more delicious way to eat healthfully."

—Marisa Moore, MBA, RDN, LD

"Everyone is invited to Maya's table! *Eating from Our Roots* is a **uniquely inclusive** approach to health via crave-worthy recipes from around the world. Maya wants everyone to know that their family food traditions can support health. In this **transformative and above all, delicious** cookbook, she points us toward a more sustainable way of eating and living."

—Jessica Jones, MS, RD, CDCES, and Wendy Lopez, MS, RD, CDCES, cofounders of Food Heaven

EATING
FROM OUR
ROOTS

goop
RODALE PRESS

NEW YORK

80+ HEALTHY HOME-COOKED
FAVORITES FROM CULTURES
AROUND THE WORLD

MAYA FELLER, MS, RD, CDN

PHOTOGRAPHS BY CHRISTINE HAN

To my late mother, Jinny Chalmers, you taught me how to love and live life fully while standing for justice. I miss you every day.

INTRODUCTION

The first time I had sugarcane freshly cut from the stalk, I was around five years old. I remember sitting with my grandfather, Simeon Alexander, in Diego Martin, Trinidad, enveloped by warm air while being kissed by the sun, sucking on sugarcane, feeling safe, loved, and without a care in the world. We would take regular drives from Diego Martin up to the countryside of Toco to visit aunties, uncles, and cousins. Somewhere along the long winding narrow roads we would stop at a stand to enjoy a hot cup of soup, always served in a Styrofoam bowl, and roasted corn wrapped in foil. I'd enjoy every bite knowing that when we arrived the aunties would have made coconut bake, dumplings, salt fish, pelau, cassava pone, bene balls, sour cherries, and so much more.

Many of my early childhood memories transport me back to visits to my grandparents' or gatherings at home in Cambridge, Massachusetts, where I grew up, with food, activism, and community at the center. I stood by and watched family and friends come together to turn out the most succulent, flavor-filled dishes, truly the best foods I have ever tasted.

During visits back to Trinidad and Tobago, food was always abundant, offered without judgment, and most often made from scratch and always with great care. These home-cooked foods provided plenty of nutrients in the most tantalizing packages. A food scientist would have dissected each dish and identified the plant-based dishes as phytonutrient- and antioxidant-rich, the poultry as free-range, and the eggs cage-free. To me and the members of my family, these foods were grown and harvested in traditional ways with methods that had been handed down over generations. The practice of growing, harvesting, and preparing food was done in a respectful way while taking the land and community into consideration. And mealtime was no different; the goal was to bring people to the table for nourishment.

My formative years were shaped with flavor, love, and curiosity. Every summer until I entered college we would travel the Caribbean, parts of western Africa, and later Australia. Instead of staying in hotels, we rented houses and spent weeks, sometimes months, living in communities with local peoples—shopping at the same grocery stores, visiting the same open-air markets, making friends with kids my age, and doing all the things that kids do. My mothers immersed our family in the local culture, and I integrated, made friends with local kids, and happily went along. As a child I never thought much about the experience of learning about culture through food and direct living with local people. It was only as an adult that

My formative years were shaped with flavor, love, and curiosity.

I understood the imprint that was left on me as I experienced slivers of life throughout the African diaspora. Those experiences deeply shaped who I am and how I think about food and culture. To be clear, we all have culture, and culture is not something assigned only to racial and ethnic minorities. Each of us was born into groups that share similar values, social norms, and histories. It is these lived and inherited experiences that contribute to our cultural backgrounds.

I learned that when you walked into a person's home, you always greeted the parents, grandparents, and other family that may have been present with a "good day" and hug. If you were invited to a meal, you washed your hands and sat with the family, ate, then helped clean up. Family meals were the norm; food took time to prepare; a colorful plate, flavor, texture, and depth were given.

During high school, my family made a number of repeat visits to Treasure Beach, St. Elizabeth Parish, Jamaica, a seaside town that was not yet overrun by developers. At that time, the oceanfront was untouched. One of those summers, we spent my birthday there. I had made friends over time, so I knew this particular birthday would be a real fete. Meals were always central to a good party, and to celebrate I wanted curried goat, a favorite of mine from an early age. With the help of friends, one of my mothers organized the purchase of a whole goat, enough for a big party with many guests and mouths to

feed. A neighbor organized a group of local fellows to prepare the goat, and a family friend organized the various cooks. Every part of the goat was utilized: the offal was used in *manishwater*, a kind of soup; the hide was dried to be used as a decorative rug; and the meat made enough curry for the whole community. It was a multigenerational gathering with joy at the center. So many celebrations were like this, with food and laughter in abundance.

After this trip I remember coming back to New York and wondering why there was such a disconnect between the foods that showed up on American plates and the origins of those foods. I was often struck by the desire to sanitize the appearance of food; skinless, boneless chicken breasts wrapped in cellophane, all perfectly uniform and placed within a food hierarchy that would be linked to a person's image of themselves.

I want to be a part of the movement that is celebrating heritage and traditional foods from cultures around the world.

Years later, I followed this thread and went to school to study clinical nutrition. I was interested in what happens to our bodies when we eat. I quickly learned that there was a set of well-researched food rules that were prescribed for people to follow in order to achieve healthy outcomes—and the people in the communities where I'd spent my childhood summers had those principles embedded in their traditional ways of eating. But something had gone awry with the way we eat in the United States.

It's no secret that rates of noncommunicable diseases such as diabetes and cardiometabolic conditions are on the rise. The United States is a sick nation. The statistics are staggering. Where I live in New York, more than 900,000 people have diabetes, and of those people, 19 percent of them do not know they have it. According to the Centers for Disease Control and Prevention, one person dies every 36 seconds in the United States as a result of a cardiometabolic disease. Only 27 percent of people living in the United States are metabolically healthy, meaning the vast majority of us are walking around with significant systemic imbalances and have no idea.

In my experience as a clinician, the concentration and incidence of high disease rates in Black, Brown, Latinx, and Indigenous communities are linked to structural and systemic inequities. Racism, not race, is the determining factor. Social determinants of health dictate how well or sick a person will be. Simply put, in the United States, communities of color are intentionally underfunded, resulting in limited access to safe, affordable, and nutritious food. Furthermore, health outcomes are impacted by where someone lives, their level of education, their access to affordable quality healthcare, and their personal safety, according to the World Health Organization. When people are denied access to the variables that are needed to express optimal health, illness is a given.

Black, Brown, Latinx, and Indigenous communities are more likely to be marginalized, encounter discrimination, and experience systemic barriers in building wealth. Because of the conditions that these communities face in the United States, data tells us that they are more likely to live in poverty and in turn be diagnosed with a noncommunicable chronic condition. There is a significant link between financial stability and access to safe and affordable nutritious foods. If a person is living paycheck to paycheck, there is no time to save for a rainy day. Crisis is often at the forefront of life. When I oversaw a New York State–funded nutrition program that served people living in poverty, I learned that having a full belly took priority over the nutrient density of a meal. If we take finances out of the equation, we know that across the board, rates of family meals are on a decline even though research supports the importance of consistent family mealtime. More of us are eating on the go and eating foods that did not come from our kitchens.

Let's talk specifically about food. The traditional foods of Black, Brown, Latinx, and Indigenous communities are health supporting, but it's because of these systemic inequities that many people in these communities have been cut off from traditional patterns of eating. Some of those traditional foods, such as avocado, kale, and quinoa, have been co-opted and have reached dominant superfood status. Meanwhile, the foods that are readily accessible to Black, Brown, Latinx, and Indigenous communities are typically nutritionally void options that supply excessive amounts of added sugars, saturated and synthetic fats, and added salts—the very foods that increase the risk of poor health outcomes and decrease the quality of life when consumed in excess on a regular and consistent basis.

With this book, I want to be a part of the movement that is celebrating heritage and traditional foods from cultures around the world. These traditional foods have often been left out of health and culinary conversations due to colonialism, white supremacy, and structural inequities, so I especially sought to highlight recipes from the African diaspora and other non-Western cultures that aren't typically a part of white American health and wellness food culture. And I also included recipes from corners of the world that are very much a part of the American health conversation—for example, the Mediterranean—but which are typically oversimplified or misunderstood. There are twenty-two nations around the Mediterranean Sea, including sections of Africa and the Middle East, and yet conversations about the health-supportive Mediterranean eating pattern typically exclude foods that aren't from a handful of European countries. Those very foods that have been excluded in haute cuisine and the healthiest food lists inherently contain ingredients and food preparation techniques that are health supporting.

I am offering you an inclusive and diverse way to think about healthy eating. I'm asking you to step away from absolute thinking and

embrace a new and different way of interacting with all foods. As you explore the regions of the globe through this book, you will learn that culture and ethnicity are not monolithic. There is so much variety and nuance among cultural groups. You may come across a dish on these pages that speaks to your heritage, as well as dishes that introduce you to ones you have yet to explore. The recipes are not an exhaustive culinary experience of the globe. Instead, I have chosen dishes from a selection of regions around the world that broaden the way that we think about healthy cooking.

I love food, flavor, and being in my kitchen. And I've developed hundreds of recipes from the lens of a dietitian. For this book I wanted to move beyond the development of healthy recipes. I wanted a collection of dishes imbued with flavor, pushing the boundaries of what I (and probably you) usually prepare. So to create the dishes in this book, I either drew from my familial and personal experiences within a particular area or consulted with a chef who has roots in or a connection to that region. During a very hot New York City summer, Chef Silvia Barban oversaw the testing of each recipe in this book in my home kitchen. In addition to recipe testing, Chef Barban helped me develop a number of the European recipes in this book and was integral in finding contributing chefs from around the globe. Chef Vanessa Cantave helped develop some of the American recipes as well as parts of the Caribbean. Chef Gerald Sombright brought his expertise to the recipes from the continent of Africa, while Chef Priyanka Naik shared Indian-inspired recipes and Chef Hong Thaimee contributed heritage Thai flavors. Chef Joel Javier shared Filipino flavors and Chef Elizabeth Falkner contributed additional American-inspired dishes.

There are aunties, uncles, and grandparents in kitchens around the world using nutritious, whole, and minimally processed ingredients in creative, flavor-maximizing ways; this book is meant as an arrow pointing you toward those ways of cooking. I intend for this book to be your first step of many in decolonizing your plate, exploring your own cultural roots around food, welcoming heritage and traditional ways of eating into your home, and discovering the amazing flavors from cultures around the world.

In my work as a registered dietitian, I practice from a lens of cultural humility. My patients are the experts in their lived experience, while I am the expert in nutrition. Together we develop sustainable patterns of eating that honor the person while taking their health goals into consideration. I know that each of us cannot be separated from who we are, that we walk with individual experiences, and that our view and experience of the world are deeply influenced by the life we have lived. My work as a provider may not directly impact systemic and structural change, since sociopolitical change happens through a combination of top-down and bottom-up shifts in policy. Public health priorities must shift, and this takes time and intention.

What I can do, however, is provide collaborative care and be a practitioner that listens to patients and honors their individuality and values and learns about their lived experiences, providing evidence-based nutrition-related care and treatment without judgment. You won't hear me telling people that there is just one "right" way to eat. Food is deeply intertwined with dominant power structures that subscribe to a one-size-fits-all approach. What does that look like in practice? You've probably seen meal plans that prescribe a lot of cottage cheese with vegetables, Greek yogurt, salads, and smoothies. All great foods, but they may not be representative of the foods eaten and loved in many foodways around the globe. What I want to do is share ways of eating the foods you already love and teach you that they are nourishing.

Research and data show that we all have better health outcomes when we consume foods lower in total amounts of added sugars, salts, and saturated and synthetic fats with a larger proportion of nutrient-dense foods in their whole and minimally processed forms the majority of the time. This does not mean we must be relegated to eating salads for eternity or, at the other extreme, animal proteins only. Time and time again, health trends encourage restrictive and self-harming behaviors in relation to food. There is a way to have a balanced healthy relationship with food while consuming a variety of foods and flavors without being absolute. In my experience, nourishment and intentional movement needs to be individualized—and I daresay we would all benefit from embracing traditional foodways.

Building a lifestyle in which you embrace the foods that you love will pay dividends in your health and well-being.

We've been told that there is one right way to eat and one way to be healthy. For the vast majority of people around the world, we've ingested a narrative about food centered on dominant ideals. Be damned if you don't eat brown rice, grilled chicken, and salad, for this is the prescription for health. The challenge is that much of this does not take ethnicity, culture, socioeconomic status, or bio-individuality into consideration. And truth be told, some of us may not want to eat brown rice, grilled chicken, and salad day after day.

To make matters worse, so many of us are no longer acquainted with the inside of our kitchens or where our food comes from. Many of us are busy and tired and need actionable, realistic, and relevant nutrition recommendations.

Health is not built on a stand-alone eating experience but rather based on patterns and habits over time. Wellness encompasses body, mind, and soul. Creating an individualized way of eating is often a nonlinear process. I frequently tell my patients that it is a radical act when they choose to prioritize themselves and make time for self-care, food, and nourishment. Prioritizing health goes against the grain. Building a lifestyle in which you embrace the foods that you love will pay dividends in your health and well-being.

HOW DOES THIS BOOK APPROACH HEALTH?

There will be no discussion of cheat meals or guilty pleasures in this book. I will not attach morality or ideas of self-worth to the act of preparing and eating food. I won't encourage restrictive patterns of eating or support shame around the foods we know and love. I will not reinforce an arbitrary hierarchy of foods. The foods that are within the pages of this book are reminiscent of the cultures from which they come and have nourished generations of people. Traditional and heritage foods from virtually all cultures around the world are built on nutrient-dense, whole, minimally processed ingredients and thus are incredibly health-supportive, but they have been left out of the dominant conversation about health. I want to restore these foods—especially those from marginalized cultures—to their rightful place at the center of a healthy pattern of eating. As a registered dietitian who is a third-culture person, and a mother raising children in a multicultural home, I want to show you how I work with my patients from diverse backgrounds to develop sustainable patterns of eating as well as how we embrace and celebrate traditions and food around my kitchen table.

With the rise of "pure" and "clean" eating in wellness culture, we have supported the narrative that health is exclusive, something that is reserved for a select few. The idea that there is only one way to eat if you wish to be healthy and pure leaves the majority behind. There is no room for non-European or Anglo-American foods when diet culture is embraced and our plates are colonized.

This myth does a great disservice to the public. There is mass confusion about how and what to eat—and even more confusion around the nuances related to prescriptive nutrition. When it comes to managing diagnoses and reducing a person's risk of adverse health outcomes, the recommendations have become even more restrictive and elitist. Additionally, the recommendations and guidelines don't account for social determinants of health or the specific variables needed to actualize health.

This cookbook is not meant to cure any health- or nutrition-related condition. I want to share my favorite flavors and textures with you and help you become acquainted with your kitchen. I've gathered recipes from around the globe because I want you to embrace the foods you love—the scents from your grandma's kitchen, the flavors from your family cookouts, the dish you crave from your favorite vacation.

Embracing and celebrating the foods you love and your cultural traditions are part of your journey to health. You'll be asked to wash, chop, grate, mince, sauté, simmer, bake, and more. Some of the dishes can be prepared in 30 minutes while others are multistep and take time, inviting you to work on them with a friend or loved one. The end result will be a taste and flavor explosion that makes you want to return to your kitchen to continue to create and explore.

You will find the intentional inclusion of recipes that call for real sugar, some salt, and fat. The deliberate and moderate use of these ingredients is notably different than purchasing a packaged good that is loaded with these ingredients. Generally, added sugars, salts, and fats should be consumed mindfully and intentionally. We don't benefit from having them at the center of our plates, but they absolutely can be a part of a healthful and balanced pattern of eating when consumed in moderation. For example, you will find a recipe for the most delicious fried chicken you will ever eat in this book. Yes, all health professionals agree, fried food should not be central in any pattern of eating; however, when consumed once in a while and in moderation, it shouldn't be detrimental to your health. Nutrition habits over time are truly what determine health outcomes.

One of the challenges I find with nutrition is that many of my patients want to be engaged in something spectacular. Balance is seen as mundane. People have come to me saying they want to actively be on a diet that promises a dazzling transformation. They believe that it will feel good, and, in the end, they can then say they have accomplished a major feat. The reality is often quite different, since diets more often than not focus on deprivation and restriction to reach an end goal. Disentangling ourselves from restrictive eating patterns and focusing on sustainable and enjoyable nourishment is liberating. Life happens, plans change. When life is happening, we must become flexible, and in this flexibility, we can find joy and excitement while experiencing new and favorite foods and still achieving health.

With my patients, I seek to find beneficial behaviors that they can replicate time and time again with minimal effort. Rather than removing food groups or drastically cutting calories for no apparent reason, we remember that nutrient-dense food in its whole and minimally processed form can and should be eaten and enjoyed on a regular basis. We also make sure that their culture stays at the forefront of their food choices and is honored without judgment.

With all that in mind, here are some pillars for you to consider as you start thinking about creating a pattern of eating that works for you.

1. There is no one size that fits all.

You are unique. Your likes, dislikes, desires, and preferences can shift and change over time. What works for your neighbor, family, or friend may not work for you. And that's 100 percent fine. The idea is to find patterns of eating that are pleasurable while supporting your health and allowing for life to happen.

2. Health exists on a spectrum.

Health does not have one definitive look. I challenge you to think about how the media and society at large portray health. Most likely an image of a young lean athletic white person comes to mind. That image could be one portrayal of health. And there is also space for images that include multiple skin tones, body shapes, sizes, genders, ages, and abilities. We need to expand how we imagine health.

3. Nothing in nutrition is absolute; it's an ever-evolving science.

Nutrition is an imperfect science, as all sciences are. Research evolves and findings change, but more important, people come to understand nutrition from their own perspective. We all have biases that are implicit and influence how we think about things. This is no different when it comes to nutrition. So take everything with a grain of salt, and operate from the ideal that there is no one size that fits all and health exists on a spectrum.

4. Shift your mindset from "What should I cut?" to "What should I add?"

We have all been indoctrinated to think about nutrition in terms of diets—namely, what we're going to cut out. Shift your thinking to focus on ways to include nutrient-dense healthful foods and health-forward behaviors into your regular patterns. Health-supporting behaviors could include working toward becoming more mindful of how often you hold your breath or how much time you spend outside when the sun is shining—as well as how often you make a meal at home.

5. Include the foods you love in your pattern of eating.

Favorite and comfort foods can and should be savored and enjoyed. We must not demonize these foods. Each of us has a favorite food. For example, seafood is my favorite food of all time, and one of my comfort foods is curry crab and dumplings from a very specific place in Tobago (Mrs. V's). I would never remove those from my pattern of eating and would be quite upset if I was told to do so. I encourage you to make space for your favorite foods in your life and on your table.

HOW TO MAKE YOUR WAY THROUGH THIS BOOK

This book will give you a taste of traditionally inspired and heritage recipes from around the world. It's loosely organized by types of foods. First are the types of foods we typically eat in the morning (porridges, baked goods, and so on), although I want to emphasize that different cultures don't necessarily share American notions of what constitutes as breakfast. I encourage you to open your mind about what counts as the first meal of the day. I then explore the rich flavors found in soups, curries, and stews. Followed by dishes where plants are the star. Many traditional recipes are built around plant foods; this is one of the ways in which getting back to our heritage offers us a pathway to health. And these plant dishes offer up layers of flavor like you've never tasted before. Next, you'll find recipes centering on fish. Many island and coastal regions rely on seafood that is naturally rich in protein as well as anti-inflammatory nutrients. And finally, meat. Meat does not need to be removed from your pattern of eating. In fact, animal proteins can be a great source of high-biological-value macronutrients, as well as micronutrients, especially for food-insecure populations. Choosing to remove animal proteins from your pattern of eating should be a matter of personal choice.

The dishes in this book will transport you around the world, and you will experience flavors from the United States, where I was born, the Caribbean and South America, Europe, the Mediterranean, parts of Africa, and farther east to Asia and the Pacific Islands. The standard American diet is known to be centered around fast and convenience foods that have lower amounts of polyphenol-rich plant foods. I have intentionally included foods from the United States not just because I'm American but also because there are health-supporting traditional foods that originated in the United States. There are dishes that use ingredients and techniques brought over by enslaved Africans, foods that originated with the Indigenous people who have lived on this land long before it was called America, and recipes that were brought over by the multitude of groups that immigrated here at different times in our history. This blending of cultures has created some incredible dishes that you should not leave off your table. I included the heritage foods of the United States to remind you that embracing your cravings while learning to listen to your internal hunger and satiety cues are all important parts of developing your pattern of eating.

This is by no means an exhaustive view of the world nor am I claiming authenticity. Some of the recipes will be familiar, others may not be. Some will feel more traditional, and others are spins on traditional foods, crafted with honor and respect. Food, like nutrition, is ever changing, and the recipes reflect that. I've also included historical tidbits about each region of the world to take a peek at how history has impacted culinary techniques and flavors.

There is a lot to learn about cooking techniques and utilizing flavor and spice when we explore and bring other food cultures into our kitchens. Soaking glutinous rice and then baking it in the oven as done in *arroz caldo* from the Philippines creates the most toothsome congee to cross your lips. Combining jaggery and turmeric with oats, as is commonly done in parts of India, makes a slightly sweet yet savory antioxidant-rich meal. Slow cooking okra, pumpkin, and coconut milk with leafy green vegetables—a phytonutrient-rich dish native to Trinidad and Tobago—makes for a creamy and hearty stew. These flavor-enhancing culinary techniques may not be standards in your current kitchen repertoire, but once learned, you can incorporate them into your routine.

STOCKING YOUR KITCHEN

The first step in cooking a meal from scratch is shopping for the ingredients. Simply going to the grocery store presents you with myriad decisions that impact not only your health but also the planet. There's a lot to consider, and while solving the challenges of agribusiness should never be placed on the individual and is beyond the scope of this book, I do want to encourage and guide you to make realistic and sustainable choices you can feel good about. Here are some principles to keep in mind as you stock your kitchen.

Understanding Processed Foods

The term *processed* is misunderstood. In the early pages of this book, I referenced nutrient-dense whole and minimally processed foods as better options for you. For the most part, this is true. Nutrient density is incredibly important and a significant part of nourishing one's body. That said, there is so much nuance that is missed when talking about processed food. All of the foods we eat are processed in some way. The act of picking an apple is a part of its processing. Cereal grains are harvested, then processed and packaged. Animal proteins are processed and made ready for consumers to purchase. The popular plant-based milks are processed. Getting our food from the farm or field to our table requires some level of processing. You may be wondering if you eat processed food, and the answer is yes, in some way, shape, or form.

When I say foods in their whole and minimally processed form, I'm referring to nutrient-dense produce, dairy, and animal proteins that have not been significantly altered as a part of their processing.

In my clinical experience, the key to understanding processed foods is being an informed and educated consumer. Reading nutrition facts and ingredient labels provides valuable information about the contents of a packaged good. It also offers you, the consumer, an opportunity to make a choice about what you put into your cart and ultimately bring to your family table. As I previously mentioned, this cookbook encourages you to return to your kitchen and peel, dice, and chop.

Think Sustainable

Sustainable farms tend to have measures in place for more humane animal farming methods and a planet-friendly approach to growing produce while also taking the health and safety of farm workers into consideration. Know this: Farmers are the heartbeat of this country and how we get *all* of our food. There is no simple rule for determining if a product was produced by sustainable farming practices, but keep reading for some tips.

Meats and Poultry

For your meats, when possible, look for organic or grass-fed and grass-finished. Grass-fed meats have a higher omega-3 fatty acid profile in comparison to corn- or grain-fed meats. When it comes to poultry and eggs, opt for pasture raised. The nutrient profile of both the chicken and egg is dependent on what the chicken is fed as well as what they graze upon. Pasture-raised eggs and poultry have a higher nutrient content of vitamin A, D, and omega-3 fatty acids in comparison to conventionally raised poultry and eggs. Organic and pasture-raised meat and poultry are frequently more expensive than their conventionally raised counterparts and not as readily accessible in some areas. When these specialty animal proteins are not available, focus on purchasing minimally processed meats and poultry.

Dairy

Dairy is fraught with controversy. I always recommend choosing dairy from farms that engage in sustainable and responsible farming practices. When possible, support your local dairy farmer and family farms. There is so much innovation happening in family farms, including a shift toward grassmilk or grass-fed and A2 dairy cows. Similar to beef, grassmilk is from cows that are pastured and grass-fed. In comparison to conventional grain- or corn-fed milk, grassmilk has a higher proportion of essential fatty acids, specifically omega-3. Whether you choose organic or conventional dairy will largely be influenced by how much you are able to spend. For my patients, I generally use the following ladder: Choose local first, then grass-fed, then organic. If none are an option, choose plain unsweetened dairy with minimal additives.

TIPS FOR INCLUDING PLANT-BASED ALTERNATIVES

You don't have to be a vegan or vegetarian to reap the health benefits of consuming plants. Current data tells us that we can all benefit from adding more plants into our regular nutrition rotation. Choosing to increase the proportion of plants on your plate or substituting one of the alternatives listed in place of an animal protein once in a while will give your body the phytonutrients and antioxidants present in the plant compounds. Most major global health agencies agree that patterns of eating that include a variety of plants provide vitamins, minerals, polyphenols, and phytonutrients that are important for whole-body health and reducing the risk of developing chronic inflammatory conditions. Eating plants consistently supports level blood sugars and healthy blood-lipid levels as well as cardiovascular health.

Plant-based alternatives can contain a number of additives that drastically shift the nutrient profile, so you need to be an informed consumer when making these choices. For anything in a box or package, read the nutrition-facts label as well as the ingredient list, and make a choice based on what you are looking for. If the alternative product is high in added sugars, perhaps you would be better served to look for an option with minimal added sugars. Same goes for the ingredient list. The first ingredient makes up the majority of the packaged good. Ingredients are listed in descending order from most to least. If the product is packed with inexpensive fillers that increase the weight of the packaged good, such as high fructose corn syrup, look for something with fewer amounts or none of these ingredients.

Some of the recipes in this book call for animal proteins, and I am well aware that there is a major push to include more plants in everyone's pattern of eating. As I said before, we can all benefit from adding more plants to our plate. If you don't eat animals or simply want to include more plants, you can use the following list as a substitution starting point.

Original	Plant-Based Alternative
BASS OR OTHER WHITE FISH FILLET	Seitan, jackfruit
BEEF, GROUND	TVP (texturized vegetable protein), lentils, crumbled tofu, black beans
BUTTER	Vegan butter (Miyoko's Creamery, Earth Balance); non-hydrogenated plant-based spread
BUTTERMILK	Soy yogurt; soy sour cream blended with unsweetened soy milk (2:1 ratio); soy milk with apple cider vinegar or lemon juice (1 cup:1 tablespoon ratio) rested for 5 minutes in refrigerator to thicken
CHEESE	Nut-based "cheese"
CHICKEN/BEEF STOCK	Vegetable stock
CHICKEN BREAST	Extra-firm or smoked tofu
CHICKEN, ROTISSERIE	Jackfruit, seitan, vital wheat gluten
CHICKEN WINGS	Mix 1½ cups vital wheat gluten, ¼ cup chickpea flour, 2 tbsp nutritional yeast, 1 tsp garlic powder, 1 tsp onion powder, 1 tsp sweet paprika, ¼ tsp salt, 1 cup vegetable broth, 1 tsp soy sauce until rubbery and firm. Bake at 350°F for 30 minutes, flip, bake for an additional 30 minutes. Remove, sear on the stovetop.
COD, SALTED	Jackfruit, brined hearts of palm
CRAB	Jackfruit, hearts of palm, artichoke hearts, tempeh
CRÈME FRAÎCHE	Soy sour cream and soy cream cheese (1:1 ratio); soy yogurt and soy cream cheese (1:1 ratio); extra-firm silken tofu and soy yogurt or soy sour cream (2:1 ratio)
EGG	Bob's Red Mill Egg Replacer, JUST Egg (plant-based), 1 tbsp flaxseed meal plus 3 tbsp water

Original	Plant-Based Alternative
FISH SAUCE	Mix ¼ cup dulse, ¼ cup dried mushrooms, 1¼ tsp miso, 1 to 2 tbsp tamari, and 1¼ cups water. Vegan fish sauce is also commercially available.
FLANK STEAK	Seitan
HAM HOCK	For umami, use amine-containing foods like mushrooms, miso, soy sauce, crumbled sheets of nori; seitan; smoked paprika for smokiness
HEAVY CREAM	Cream of coconut; soy half-and-half, melted non-hydrogenated plant-based spread, unsweetened soy milk (1:1:2 ratio)
HERRING OR KIPPERS, SMOKED	Smoked eggplant or mushrooms
LANGOUSTINE	Lobster mushroom
MILK, WHOLE	Coconut milk, soy milk, unsweetened nut milk
PORK, GROUND	Lentils, crumbled firm tofu
PORK LIVER	Seitan marinated in beetroot juice and soy sauce
PORK TENDERLOIN	Mushrooms (portobello, chanterelle)
RED SNAPPER	Jackfruit, seitan
SAUSAGE, ANDOUILLE	Plant-based andouille sausages, mushrooms with smoked paprika
SAUSAGE, ITALIAN	Plant-based Italian sausages, mushrooms
SCALLOPS	King oyster mushrooms
SEAFOOD STOCK	Stock made with sesame oil, dried seaweed, kombu, mushroom seasoning, dried mushrooms
SHRIMP	Konjak root
SPAM	Smoked tofu
YOGURT	Plant-based yogurt

Picking produce

First and foremost, focus on having fruits and vegetables as a consistent part of your pattern of eating. Similar to dairy, I always recommend supporting local farmers' markets, farm shares, community-supported agriculture, and local produce subscription boxes as much as possible. Shopping this way gives you access to the freshest and most delicious seasonal produce. Having access to organic or conventional produce is influenced by where you live and by what you can afford. If you can't get organic produce, make sure you eat fruits and veggies regularly; that's what really matters. If you live in an area where green markets are a part of the culture, join in. Make it a part of your routine and get to know the farmers.

Produce can be fresh, frozen, canned, boxed, and jarred. If your produce is not fresh, read the labels and make a choice based on your needs.

Choosing oils

People have a lot of questions when it comes to oil. Is the oil refined or unrefined; what's the ratio of monounsaturated versus polyunsaturated fats versus saturated fats; does the oil have a high smoke point or low cook point? I could go on, but what you really want to know is: What does all of this mean when I'm in the kitchen, and how will it impact my health?

Oils are among the most malleable and regularly utilized functional components in the culinary world, and almost any plant can be processed to make oil. Oils can transfer heat and create a crispy exterior while leaving the center tender. They enhance flavor as well as modify the consistency of your favorite dish. Generally, oils should be stored in a cool dark area to preserve quality and flavor and used within a year of purchase.

As for choosing the right oil, often the cooking method determines the type of oil that will work the best. Different varieties of oils are used for dressings, baking, and frying. Let's use the smoke point as an example. The smoke point of an oil is the temperature at which fats and oils begin to degrade or break down. And with that breakdown, there is the potential for the development of unwanted by-products. You will notice that avocado oil shows up in many recipes; this is because of its high smoke point and stability at higher temperatures.

Vegetable-based oils are extracted from plants and sometimes refined. Extraction happens in one of three ways: cold-pressing, expeller-pressing, or chemical solvents. Before you get too excited, know that these processes are not new. Cold-pressing is what it sounds like; it involves mechanical pressing of seeds against a press. These oils are often unrefined and retain the full flavor of the original plant—and carry a higher price point. Expeller-pressing generates heat because the seeds are pressed at extremely high pressures. Here, most of the nutrients, aroma, color, and flavor are retained. Lastly, extraction with chemical solvents involves mechanically pressing the seeds in combination with a food-grade solvent to ensure that the maximum amount of oil is extracted from the seeds.

Whatever method of extraction is used, the oil may then go on to be refined; if it's not, it's called unrefined oil. Refining removes unwanted impurities, including water, resins, gums, soil, free fatty acids, and color compounds, resulting in a more neutral and mild-flavored oil. Unrefined oils are robust and bursting with flavor, but they are not as shelf stable and have a lower smoke point. Refined oils are better suited for high-heat cooking above 400°F.

And what about saturated fat? We generally talk about saturation in relation to how heart-healthy an oil is. The less saturated, the better for cardiovascular health. Unsaturated fatty acids, which include monounsaturated and polyunsaturated fatty acids, are found in olive oil, avocado oil, and sunflower seed oil, among others.

I recommend opting for plant-based oils in place of animal-based fats the majority of the time and leaning into unsaturated oils in place of saturated oils. The oils in the following chart are widely available and have varying amounts of monounsaturated and polyunsaturated fatty acids. Their nutrient profiles differ as well as the amounts of omega-3 and omega-6 fatty acids. They in turn have different impacts on health. I recommend varying the oils that are used for cooking and finishing dishes as this diversifies what you are exposed to.

REFINED OILS

Name	Description/Uses	Fat Type*	Smoke Point
ALMOND	Nut oils are best used in cold dishes; heat can reduce their delicate flavor.	Mono	495°F (257°C)
AVOCADO	Avocado oil is a light, slightly nutty-tasting oil.	Mono	520°F (271°C)
CANOLA	Of all oils, canola is second highest in monounsaturated fatty acid content. (Olive oil has more, but its flavor is not as mild.) Refined canola oil's mild flavor and relatively high smoke point making it a good all-purpose oil.	Mono	400°F (204°C)
OLIVE	Olive oil is a monounsaturated oil extracted from tree-ripened olives. Olive oils range from light amber to green in color and bland to extremely strong in flavor. Olive oil is graded according to its degree of acidity and the process used to extract the oil.	Mono	Unrefined: 320°F (160°C) Extra-virgin: 406°F (208°C) Virgin: 420°F (216°C) Extra-light: 468°F (242°C)
PEANUT	Peanut oil is made from pressed, steam-cooked peanuts. Peanut oil has a light, nutty flavor and can tolerate high heat.	Mono	450°F (232°C)
SAFFLOWER	Safflower oil is an all-purpose oil made from the seeds of safflowers. Safflower oil remains liquid when chilled, and it has a yellow color and mild flavor. The refined version has a high resistance to rancidity.	Mono	450°F (232°C)
SESAME	There are two types of sesame oil made from pressed sesame seeds: light (made with untoasted sesame seeds) and dark (made with toasted sesame seeds). Light sesame oil has a nutty flavor and is especially good for frying. Dark sesame oil has a stronger flavor and is generally only used in small quantities for flavoring foods. It has a smoky, sesame aroma; nutty taste; dark-brown color; thick consistency; and cloudy appearance.	Poly	410°F (210°C)
SOYBEAN	This oil is an all-purpose oil because of its neutral flavor. High-oleic soybean oil is widely available, and most vegetable oil blends contain soybean oil. Highly refined soybean oil is reasonably priced, very mild, and versatile, accounting for more than 80% of all oil used in commercial food production in the US.	Poly (46%) Mono (40%)	492°F (256°C)
SUNFLOWER	Sunflower oil is a mild, all-purpose oil made from sunflower seeds. The nutrient profile varies based on the linoleic and oleic acid content.	Mono	450°F (232°C)

*Type refers here to the predominant fatty acid in the oil. All vegetable oils contain a combination of saturated, monounsaturated, and polyunsaturated fatty acids. The amount and type of fatty acid will vary based on the oil as do their nutrition profiles and health benefits.

Choosing sweeteners and added sugars

Added sugars are another major area of global discussion. The World Health Organization (WHO) has dedicated countless hours and resources to encourage countries around the globe to enact policies that support reducing added sugars in packaged goods. The organization notes that a large majority of the added sugars that are consumed are hidden in packaged goods. And the American Heart Association (AHA) further backs this up and calls out the major sources of added sugars as sugar-sweetened beverages, fruit drinks, candy, and packaged baked goods.

Added sugars or free sugars do not include naturally occurring sugars that are present in fruits, vegetables, and unsweetened dairy products. The recommendation from the WHO is to have no more than 5 percent of total energy intake coming from added sugars. This recommendation is so strong because of the association between high added-sugar intake and the increased risk of developing diabetes and other cardiometabolic conditions. They are telling us all to slow down on the sugar. In the United States, the average adult consumes the equivalent of seventeen teaspoons or 71 grams of added sugar each day! More than twice the recommended amount. The WHO recommends no more than six teaspoons of added/free sugars each day.

Opting to prepare your own meals and modulate any added sugars gives you a step up when it comes to long-term health. Some people choose to consider alternatives such as date, coconut palm, or maple sugar, as they have lower glycemic indexes than white table sugar. They are still sweeteners, so you will need to make an informed choice about how and when you use them.

Stock your pantry with spices and staples

Herbs and spices have significant medicinal properties including anticarcinogenic, antitumorigenic activities as well as the ability to help lower blood lipids and blood sugars. Not only do they contribute meaningful antioxidants and nutrients, but they are also an incredible way of infusing a dish with flavor. As you move through this book you may come across some lesser-used herbs and spices. They impart incredible, distinct flavors. Following is a short list and description of some of them. Use them in the recipes in this book. Then, experiment on your own.

Kombu

Kombu is a type of edible seaweed used in many Japanese dishes. Kombu is high in an amino acid, glutamic acid, which is responsible for the umami flavor. It can be found dried, pickled, or fresh. The main use of kombu is in the Japanese stock soup kombu dashi. I often recommend using kombu as a texturizer for dry beans, since the amino acids found in kombu can help make beans more digestible.

Dashi

Dashi is a staple base in Japanese cooking, similar to a vegetable broth. Dashi powder is a combination of steeped kombu, a dried kelp, and *katsuobushi*, a dried and aged tuna that gives a savory, umami flavor to many dishes.

Berbere

Berbere is the Ethiopian word for "pepper." Berbere is a fiery spice blend that typically includes both whole spice seeds and ground spices. The flavor backbone is provided by chili peppers and complemented with other spices such as black pepper, fenugreek, coriander, cinnamon, cardamom, and cloves.

Vadouvan

Vadouvan can be best described as the French version of curry powder. *Vadouvan* typically contains spices such as fenugreek, cumin, cardamom, and mustard seeds, though there are many different versions of the blend. It differs from curry powder in that it contains aromatics such as shallots and garlic, whereas curry powder typically relies on dried spices.

Tamarind

The word *tamarind* comes from the Arabic words *tamar hind,* which mean "Indian date." Although indigenous to the savannas of Africa, tamarind is an integral spice in Indian, Southeast Asian, and Central and South American cuisine as well as across the Caribbean and has a sweet yet tangy flavor.

Togarashi

Togarashi, also known as Japanese seven-spice powder, is composed of a variety of ingredients depending on local and regional tradition or the preferences of the cook. Traditionally, it contains chili, orange peel, seaweed, ginger, poppy seeds, and sesame seeds.

Star anise

Shaped like a star, star anise is a seedpod from the Chinese evergreen plant native to southwest China and Vietnam. It is an integral ingredient in Middle Eastern, Vietnamese, Chinese, and Indian cuisine. To some, the flavor is reminiscent of anise. Although the flavor is commonly thought of as sweet, it is often used in savory dishes.

HOW TO MODIFY RECIPES FOR HEALTH CONDITIONS

You may be asking yourself how you can enjoy some of the recipes in this cookbook if you have a diagnosis of a chronic disease such as diabetes, high blood pressure, or high cholesterol that requires you to make mindful choices around food. I'm here to tell you that you can enjoy them with intentional modifications. Before we get to the modifications, it's important to know and understand that having a diagnosis of a condition like diabetes or a cardiometabolic condition is just that, a diagnosis. For those reading this section who do not have a diagnosis, understand that blaming a person for having a health condition is not productive. Having diabetes or high blood pressure does not define the person; rather it informs the potential prescriptive nature of food, nutrition, and lifestyle they may take on. Living with a diagnosis requires intentional interaction with food and conscious choices. To be clear, this does not mean randomly cutting out foods but instead making choices that are individualized with health in mind.

Recommended modifications by cardiometabolic condition

Disorders of glucose metabolism

People living with diabetes, prediabetes, or insulin resistance have a hard time metabolizing and utilizing sugars coming from foods. There is no specific "diabetes diet," but there are patterns of eating that are diabetes friendly. It may sound the same, but it's not. Diabetes-friendly patterns of eating support level blood sugars and reduce the risk of developing additional metabolic imbalances. As with any nutrition prescription, it must be individualized. People who have diabetes or who are at an increased risk of developing diabetes benefit from focusing on carbohydrate literacy and include patterns of eating that are abundant in fiber and nutrient-rich vegetables, fruits, and whole grains in place of refined sugars and grains. (The same recommendations apply to the general public.) For the purposes of this book, readers who are concerned about their carbohydrate intake may want to be mindful of portion sizes and think about how to round out meals that have a larger proportion of starch with a nonstarchy vegetable side as a way to increase the quantity of fiber on the plate as well as adding a source of protein to support level blood sugars.

Hypertension (high blood pressure)

For those who are salt sensitive, reducing added salts can support the reduction of blood pressure. This is an opportunity to make your own broths for any recipe that calls for a broth or stock. If you opt to purchase store-bought broths, choosing a low-sodium version will support healthy blood pressure levels. Additionally, enjoying an abundance of phytonutrient- and antioxidant-rich vegetables, fruits, and whole grains helps reduce oxidative stress. You can always incorporate an extra serving of vegetables or fruit of your choice to any recipe or enjoy them as a side.

Disorders of lipid metabolism (high cholesterol, dyslipidemia)

Choosing monounsaturated and polyunsaturated fats, especially the ones that are liquid at room temperature and come from plants, are an integral part of supporting healthy lipid levels within the blood. Being mindful of the quantity and frequency of use further supports healthy cholesterol levels. Extra-virgin olive oil appears in a number of recipes and is loved for its heart-healthy monounsaturated fatty acid profile. Fiber and antioxidants provide further support when thinking about blood lipid profile, similar to the recommendations for disorders of glucose metabolism. Incorporating whole and ancient grains along with a color-filled pattern of eating further supports healthy lipid levels. Additionally, if you are eating with heart health in mind, you can opt to swap in a plant-based oil or non-hydrogenated plant-based spread in place of an animal fat.

I hope this introduction has provided a window as well as a mirror into alternative ways of framing conversations around health and nutrition. Additionally, I hope you feel motivated to jump into exploration within your kitchen. This next section is where the magic, joy, and fun happens—you will be the creator of delicious meals. You will be exposed to—and encouraged to make—some of my favorite meals and hopefully find some new favorites that will become a part of your rotation. You'll travel the globe and learn a bit about the intersection of history, culture, and food all while honing your kitchen skills.

Wishing you all good food along with joy and laughter in the kitchen!

PORRIDGE, TOASTS & BAKED GOODS

1

GRIDDLECAKES *(Northeast)*

Griddlecakes were a staple in my home growing up and one of the first recipes I learned to make on my own. We always made them with yogurt rather than milk and used whole-grain flours long before it was cool. The batter can be made in advance and stored in the refrigerator for up to 3 days, allowing you to have a quick warm breakfast with little to no fuss.

1 cup all-purpose einkorn flour

½ cup almond flour

½ teaspoon baking powder

1 cup vanilla whole-milk low-sugar yogurt

2 large eggs

1 tablespoon non-hydrogenated plant-based butter

For the berry compote

1 (15-ounce) bag frozen mixed berries

1 pink lemon or Meyer lemon, peeled and cut into chunks

2 tablespoons pomegranate molasses

Nutrition Tip: Thinking about your blood sugars? You can substitute date syrup in place of pomegranate molasses for a lower-glycemic alternative that won't produce such a rapid spike in blood sugars.

Ingredient Highlight: Einkorn flour is an ancient grain bursting with many essential nutrients. In comparison to conventional flour, einkorn has a lower gluten content so may be better tolerated by those with a gluten sensitivity.

Place the einkorn and almond flours and baking powder in a large mixing bowl and create a well in the center.

Place the yogurt and eggs in the well and whisk together with a fork. Let the batter sit for 5 to 10 minutes to activate the baking powder.

Heat a large cast-iron skillet over medium heat and add the plant-based butter. Ladle in ¼ cup of the batter and cook about 3 minutes, or until the sides of the pancake curl up. Flip and cook about 3 minutes, or until golden brown.

Make the berry compote: In a small pot over medium-low heat, add the berries, lemon, and molasses, and cook for 15 minutes, stirring often.

Serve the pancakes with berry compote and enjoy!

I grew up in **the Northeast**, a region of the United States steeped in complicated and painful history. Over the past three centuries, people from around the globe have colonized as well as migrated to the Northeastern US, but before that the land was home to Indigenous people who cultivated the land, hunted animals, and gathered a wide variety of foods that were readily and seasonally available—squash, beans, deer, fish, berries, and roots and tubers. First Nations peoples continue to have a thriving cultural and culinary influence that can be seen today in what we mistakenly think of as traditional American foods—for example, griddlecakes.

BISCUITS *(American South)*

WITH BLACKBERRY CAYENNE JAM
AND CHAMOMILE BUTTER

Many cultures have their own versions of biscuits, each delicious in its own way. The biscuits from regions within the American South are known for their light yet buttery flavor—and loved by all. This is an homage to those well-loved biscuits with an ingredient twist. The combination of whole wheat and einkorn flours changes the nutrient profile by increasing the fiber and mineral content, and they're topped with a sweet kick from the jam and floral butter.

1 cup whole wheat flour, plus more for kneading the dough

2 cups all-purpose einkorn flour

½ teaspoon salt

4 teaspoons baking powder

½ teaspoon cream of tartar

12 tablespoons (1½ sticks) unsalted butter, chilled, plus 3 tablespoons (optional), melted, for brushing

1 large egg

1 cup buttermilk, chilled

Jam (recipe follows), for serving

Coated butter (recipe follows), for serving

Nutrition Tip: If you are being mindful of your blood lipid levels, then opt for buttermilk in place of whole milk. Buttermilk contains less total fat in comparison to whole milk and is excellent when baking.

Ingredient Highlight: Cayenne peppers—known for their spice—contain the bioactive compound capsaicin, which has been researched for its anticarcinogenic properties.

Preheat the oven to 450°F. Line a sheet pan with parchment paper and set aside.

Sift the flours, salt, baking powder, and cream of tartar into a large mixing bowl and whisk together.

Using a box grater, grate the 12 tablespoons butter directly into the dry ingredients, stopping after a few passes to ensure the shreds are coated in the flour mixture and not sticking together. Be careful not to handle the butter too much or it will start to melt.

In a separate small bowl, gently whisk the egg and buttermilk together.

Add the egg-milk mixture to the dry ingredients and stir until just combined. If your butter has started to melt, place the dough in the refrigerator for 10 minutes before moving on to the next step.

Turn your dough onto a lightly floured work surface. Knead the dough gently about 10 times into a large disk. Your dough should be 1 inch thick. Using a 2-inch biscuit cutter or the rim of a drinking glass, cut the biscuits and place onto the prepared sheet pan.

Bake for 12 to 15 minutes, until the biscuits just start to become golden brown. Remove them from the oven. If you'd like, you can brush the tops with a generous amount of melted butter.

Serve immediately with jam and coated butter.

Recipe continues

FOR THE JAM

1 (10-ounce) bag frozen blackberries

¼ teaspoon cayenne pepper

Zest of 1 lemon

Juice of ½ lemon

3 tablespoons date syrup

Place the blackberries, cayenne, lemon zest, lemon juice, and date syrup in a medium pot over low heat and cook for 30 minutes, stirring occasionally.

Remove the pot from the heat and carefully transfer the jam to a heat-safe bowl. Blend with a hand mixer, pulsing for 15 to 30 seconds.

FOR THE COATED BUTTER

4 tablespoons (½ stick) unsalted butter, at room temperature

½ cup finely chopped fresh chamomile, or ¼ cup finely chopped dried chamomile flowers

Place the butter in a small mixing bowl and coat with the chamomile. Gently toss until all of the butter is coated. Once the butter is completely coated, cut it into 12 pats.

Serve the butter with the biscuits.

 **BAMMY** *(Jamaica)*

Bammy is an unleavened cassava-based bread that is traditionally made with fresh cassava root and soaked in coconut milk, then pan-fried. For this version I've used cassava flour that is more readily available and easier to manipulate but still gluten-free for those who are in need of this option. Bammy is delicious alongside eggs, ackee—a fruit with an egglike texture—or Salted Cod (page 172).

1½ cups cassava flour

½ teaspoon kosher salt

1 (13.5-ounce) can full-fat coconut milk

¼ cup avocado oil, plus more as needed

Nutrition Tip: Cassava flour has an intermediate glycemic index value and can be enjoyed in moderation as well for those being mindful of reducing fluctuations in blood sugars.

In a medium mixing bowl, combine the flour and salt. Add the coconut milk and mix well until all the ingredients are combined and form a dough.

With clean hands, separate the dough into ice-cream-scoop-size balls, roll the balls between the palms of your hands, and flatten the balls into ½-inch-thick disks.

Heat a medium frying pan over medium-low heat. Once the pan is hot, add the oil and dough. Pan-fry the bammies for 7 minutes on each side, until golden brown. Add additional oil to the pan if needed.

Serve with Jamaican-Style Callaloo (page 111) or Trinidadian-style (see page 114), or Salted Cod (page 172) and scrambled eggs.

MUSHROOM, CHIVE, AND CHEDDAR WAFFLES *(Central US)*

As you move through regions in the US, waffles may be served with sweet and savory options most often for breakfast or brunch. With the addition of nutrient-rich mushrooms and chives, these savory waffles can be enjoyed at any meal of the day. If you are feeling adventurous, top the waffles with some wilted greens and the chili oil or garlic of your choice.

1 cup all-purpose einkorn flour

¾ cup whole wheat flour

1 teaspoon baking powder

1 teaspoon kosher salt

2 large eggs, separated

1 cup buttermilk

4 tablespoons (½ stick) unsalted non-hydrogenated plant-based butter, melted and cooled

1 cup grated aged Wisconsin Cheddar cheese

¾ cup diced cremini mushrooms

⅓ cup diced chives

Calabrian chili peppers in oil (optional)

Maple syrup or honey (optional)

Ingredient Highlight: Chives—along with other allium vegetables such as onions, garlic, leeks, and shallots—are rich in phytochemicals that blunt free radical damage. Studies have shown that eating them one to two times a week reduces the risk of developing certain types of cancers.

In a small bowl, combine the flours, baking powder, and salt. Set aside

In a medium bowl, whisk the egg whites by hand or with a mixer until soft peaks form. Set aside.

In a large bowl, whisk together the egg yolks and buttermilk. Gradually add the dry ingredients to the egg yolk–milk mixture until combined. Slowly add the butter to the mixture and whisk until fully incorporated, then add ¾ cup of cold water and whisk just until combined. Do not overmix the batter. If your batter is too thick, add more cold water, 1 tablespoon at a time, until it has a consistency similar to honey.

Add the cheese, mushrooms, and chives, then use a rubber spatula to gently fold them into the batter. Finally, add the reserved egg whites and again gently fold them in until your batter is fully combined.

Heat your waffle iron. Cook the waffles according to the waffle maker's directions. For a spicy addition to this savory dish, top each waffle with 1 finely chopped Calabrian chili and ¼ cup of maple syrup (if using). Serve immediately.

Waffles crossed the ocean and made their way to the US in the early 1600s with Dutch colonists. Home cooks have customized and perfected their own versions over centuries. **The central part of the US** is an important agricultural hub, contributing significant amounts of corn, soybeans, and wheat to the US food supply—foods that show up in many people's favorite meals.

SAVORY FRENCH TOAST *(India)*

This is not your average French toast. It's stuffed with vegetables, nuts, and spices, making it a plant-forward delight. The first time I tried it, I stamped my foot, said, "I'm not mad at this at all," and proceeded to devour it. It is an excellent way to utilize any day-old bread and has a smoky sausage-like flavor despite not containing meat! The recipe calls for ketchup; don't turn your nose up at that condiment—it adds something extra special to the eating experience.

1 tablespoon plus 2 teaspoons non-hydrogenated plant-based spread

½ small red onion, diced

2 large eggs

2 serranos or Indian green chilies, seeded and diced

2 tablespoons chopped fresh cilantro leaves

½ teaspoon ground cumin

⅛ teaspoon kosher salt

4 slices whole wheat sourdough bread, crust trimmed off

1 lemon, quartered for garnish

Pinch of chaat masala, for garnish

Maple syrup, for serving

Ketchup, for serving

Note: Chaat masala can be purchased online.

Prep Tip: Save the crusts to make bread crumbs!

For the cashew cream

½ cup raw unsalted cashews, soaked in warm water for at least 1 hour

½ teaspoon fresh lemon juice

Pinch of kosher salt

¼ teaspoon ground cumin

1 tablespoon sour cream, at room temperature

In a large saucepan over medium heat, sauté 1 tablespoon of the plant-based spread and the onions. Sauté for 8 to 10 minutes, until the onions are slightly caramelized. Set aside.

Make the cashew cream: Place the cashews (including their soaking water), lemon juice, salt, cumin, sour cream, and ¼ cup of water into a high-speed blender or food processor, and blend on high until smooth and creamy. Set aside.

Make the batter: In a shallow and wide bowl, whisk together the eggs, chilies, cilantro, caramelized onion, cumin, and salt. Set aside.

Spread a spoonful of the cashew cream in between 2 slices of the bread. Carefully dip the bread into the egg mixture until generously coated, making sure to coat all sides. Set aside on a parchment-lined plate. Repeat for the other slices.

Heat a medium cast-iron skillet over medium-high heat. Once the skillet is hot, add 1 teaspoon of the non-hydrogenated plant-based spread. Once the spread is melted and bubbly, add the battered

Recipe continues

bread. Reduce the heat to medium-low. Cook 2 to 4 minutes on each side, until golden brown. Remove and repeat with the remaining bread.

Place the French toast on a platter, and while hot, immediately squeeze some fresh lemon juice and sprinkle on chaat masala (if using) so it sticks to the French toast. Serve drizzled with maple syrup and ketchup on the side.

Ingredient Highlight: Non-hydrogenated plant-based spread is a fantastic alternative to margarine or other hydrogenated spreads. Depending on the manufacturer, many have added plant sterols that add extra cardioprotective properties.

GALETTE BRETONNE *(France)*

Serves 6

(BUCKWHEAT CREPE) WITH ASPARAGUS, SMOKED TROUT ROE, AND EGG

Galette Bretonne is a savory buckwheat crepe that is often made with ham and egg but can be easily adapted to suit your palette. This version leans into vegetables and seafood for a heart-healthy twist. Simple to put together, it's not just a breakfast food—you can enjoy it any time of the day.

Kosher salt and freshly ground black pepper to taste

12 medium asparagus spears, cut into thirds

1 cup oat milk

9 large eggs

⅔ cup buckwheat flour

½ cup all-purpose flour

4 tablespoons non-hydrogenated plant-based spread

1 (3-ounce) jar smoked trout roe, for garnish

1 bunch fresh tarragon, torn, for garnish

Prep Tip: The batter for the crepes can be made in advance and stored in an airtight container in the refrigerator for up to 3 days.

Ingredient Highlight: Asparagus is a great source of kaempferol and quercetin polyphenols and flavonoids. These compounds are beneficial as they have the potential to be protective and reduce oxidation due to their antiradical capacity.

In a medium stockpot, bring 6 cups of water to a boil over high heat. Add a pinch of salt and the asparagus and cook for 2 minutes. Meanwhile, set up an ice bath in a large bowl. Remove the asparagus spears from the water and place in the ice bath for 10 minutes, until they cool down. (This helps the asparagus retain its vibrant green color.)

While the asparagus is cooling, make the crepes. In a medium mixing bowl, whisk the oat milk, 3 of the eggs, and ⅓ cup of water together. Add the flours and continue to whisk until well combined.

Heat a 12-inch nonstick skillet or a seasoned 7- or 8-inch crepe pan over medium heat. Brush the pan with non-hydrogenated plant-based spread, and when the pan is hot, remove from the heat and ladle in about 3 tablespoons of batter. Tilt or swirl the pan to distribute the batter evenly, and return to the heat.

Cook for about 1 minute, or until you can easily loosen the edges with a spatula. Flip and cook on the other side for 30 seconds. Brush the pan again with non-hydrogenated plant-based spread and continue until all of the spread and batter is used. Place the crepes on a plate with a warm wet towel on top.

In the same pan, add 1 tablespoon non-hydrogenated plant-based spread and cook the remaining 6 eggs until done to your preference. Then add the asparagus on the side to heat slightly and season with black pepper.

To serve, place the asparagus and eggs at the center of the crepes and top with trout roe and fresh tarragon, then gently fold the edges toward the egg to create a square shape.

BAKED GOODS, ETC.

53

COCONUT BAKE *(Trinidad and Tobago)*

A type of quick bread sometimes called Johnnycake, this bake is enjoyed in many Caribbean islands and reminds me of my grandmother's house. It can be baked or fried, and for this recipe, I've chosen to bake it and add coconut. I suggest enjoying it with salt fish, callaloo, and ripe avocado.

1½ cups white bread flour, plus more for rolling the dough

1½ cups whole wheat bread flour

2 tablespoons baking powder

Pinch of kosher salt

½ cup non-hydrogenated plant-based spread

¾ cup unsweetened coconut flakes

1⅔ cups full-fat coconut milk

Preheat the oven to 375°F. Line a sheet pan with parchment paper.

In a large bowl, combine the flours, baking powder, salt, and plant-based spread. Mix the ingredients until just combined and crumbly. Add the coconut flakes and coconut milk slowly, while working the dough into a ball.

Place the dough on a lightly floured surface and roll into a 1-inch-thick circle. Prick the dough with a fork to make a design. Transfer to the prepared sheet pan and bake for 25 to 30 minutes, until golden. Remove from the oven and allow to sit until the bread reaches room temperature.

To serve, slice and enjoy with salt fish and either Jamaican-Style Callaloo (page 111) or Trinidadian-style (page 114).

Nutrition Tip: If you are managing blood sugars, consider using only whole wheat flour to increase the whole-grain content of the bake. Whole grains are absorbed more slowly into the bloodstream and produce less of a spike in blood sugars compared to refined grains.

Ingredient Highlight: Coconut milk is a great plant-based source of medium-chain triglycerides. Recommendations around coconut and coconut products are sometimes controversial, as they contain saturated fats that are plant based. Original research notes that saturated fats are among the primary drivers of cardiovascular disease. The evidence for coconut products remains mixed.

The food scene of Trinidad and Tobago can hardly be considered a "fusion." Instead, it is its own cuisine entirely. A multicultural nation with diverse ethnicities and religions, you can find influences from the indigenous Amerindians, Africa, China, Europe, and India in the heritage dishes native to Trinidad and Tobago.

Originally colonized by Christopher Columbus in 1498, the country of Trinidad and Tobago is a dual-island nation located between the Caribbean Sea and the North Atlantic ocean. Following Spanish occupation, the islands were under British control in the early nineteenth century, a time when sugar and cocoa production dominated the market.

Popular African-influenced dishes include roasted meat, stews, and Pelau (page 186), a mixture of pigeon pies, rice, and meat with coconut and pepper. Callaloo (Granny's Callaloo on page 114 or Jamaica-Style Callaloo on page 111)—a thick souplike meal made of greens, okra, and crab—has been around for decades, a dish created by enslaved Africans when the islands were under Spanish rule. Popular East Indian fare includes *paratha*, Indian bread with masala-based curries, and *doubles*, chickpeas served in fried bread, or *bara*. The best known of these dishes are possibly roti and *dahl puri*, a form of Indian *chapatti*, a flour-based or split pea flatbread eaten with stews, vegetables, and curries.

Chinese, Middle Eastern, and Spanish cuisines are also found within the borders. A popular dish near the beach is "shark and bake," a fried shark sandwich with a pepper sauce consisting of tamarind, garlic, and a local herb called *shado beni* (*culantro*). Seafood is plentiful in the cuisine as well as fruits and vegetables—like citrus fruits, sour cherries, avocados, cassava, yams, and dasheen bush—that grow bountifully in the tropical climate. Other unique local produce includes sapodillas, *pommecythere*, eddoes, and tanias.

KHUBZ *(Middle East + North Africa)*

(Flatbread)

Don't be frightened by making bread. It can be really easy with the right recipe; in fact, this one has only four ingredients. It's simple to make and incredibly appetizing. The combination of vitamin-rich whole grains and spices helps promote beneficial gut bacteria. This very quick flatbread pairs nicely with Mezze (page 125) and can mop up Hummus with Black Sesame Tahini (page 128) like a champion.

2 teaspoons active dry yeast

2½ cups whole wheat bread flour, plus more for rolling the dough

¼ cup olive oil, plus more to coat the bowl

1 cup za'atar

Hummus (see page 128) or mezze of your choice (see page 125), for serving

Note: This bread is inspired by traditional za'atar–topped Manakish.

Nutrition Tip: Whole wheat flour is less refined and is a good source of B vitamins as well as minerals. It also has a low glycemic index and will not cause your blood-sugar levels to rapidly rise, and it's a great alternative to all-purpose flour when needed.

In a medium bowl, combine the yeast with 1 cup of warm water and mix.

In a stand mixer fitted with the dough hook attachment, combine the flour and water mixture. Mix on medium speed for 3 to 5 minutes, until the dough comes together. Cover the dough and let it rest at room temperature for a minimum of 30 minutes, ideally 60 minutes.

On a lightly floured surface, pat the dough down and cut into 8 equal pieces. Roll each piece of dough out until ½ inch thick.

Heat a 9-inch skillet over medium heat. When the pan is very hot, add the oil and 1 piece of the rolled dough and cook for 60 to 70 seconds on one side. Flip and season with 2 tablespoons of za'atar. Cook for another minute, until golden brown, flip, reduce heat to medium-low, and cook another 60 to 90 seconds on the other side. Repeat the process for the remaining 7 pieces of dough.

To serve, pair the flatbread with hummus or any mezze of your choice.

PAO DE QUEIJO *(Brazil)*
(CHEESE BREAD)

Tapioca drinks may be trending, but if you haven't tried this tapioca bread, you must. It's divine, with a perfect crispy exterior. The combination of sweet ripe banana and the saltiness of sharp cheese makes for a full-flavored complement. This recipe adds banana, an excellent way to impart sweetness. This is a fun twist on the classic savory style.

½ cup whole milk

½ cup unsweetened almond milk

½ cup avocado oil

½ teaspoon kosher salt

2 cups tapioca starch (flour)

2 large eggs

1 ripe banana, mashed

¾ cup sharp Cheddar cheese, grated

Coffee or blended fruit, for serving

Chef's Note: Use block cheese rather than pregrated cheeses. Grating your cheese results in a more flavorful cheese bread.

Nutrition Tip: If supporting healthy blood lipid levels is top of mind, you can increase your plant intake by using only unsweetened almond milk in this recipe.

Preheat the oven to 350°F. Line a sheet pan with parchment paper. Set aside.

In a medium saucepan over medium heat, heat the milks, oil, and salt just until bubbles start to form around the edges. Immediately turn off the heat. Add the tapioca starch and stir until just combined and the starch has been absorbed by the liquid.

Transfer the hot dough to a stand mixer fitted with the paddle attachment. Gradually mix going between low and medium speeds for about 5 minutes, or until the dough is smooth. Allow the dough to cool for 5 to 7 minutes before proceeding to the next step.

In a small bowl, whisk the eggs and banana. Add half of the egg mixture to the stand mixer. Mix at medium speed for 2 to 3 minutes, until fully incorporated. Add the remaining egg mixture and mix until fully incorporated. The dough will be sticky with small lumps.

Add the cheese all at once and mix at medium speed until the cheese is fully incorporated and the dough pulls away from the wall of the mixing bowl and forms a ball.

Shape the dough into balls using about 1 tablespoon of dough per ball—a scoop works great here. Transfer the prepared dough balls to the sheet pan lined with parchment paper.

Bake for 30 to 35 minutes, until the bread is puffed and golden with specks of melted cheese. Be careful not to underbake the bread; it should have a nice gentle crunch on the outside and a chewy but not raw cheesy center. Remove from the oven and allow it to cool.

To serve, enjoy with coffee or blended fruit for breakfast.

BREAKFAST TOCILOG (the Philippines)

(CURED PORK, FRIED RICE, AND FRIED EGG)

Chef Joel says, "It's always an extra-special day when it begins with this dish," and he remarked that Filipinos love hearty breakfasts that provide sustenance to start the day off with a an explosion of flavor—and this dish fits the order. The tantalizing components of this protein-rich breakfast—sweet cured pork called TO-ci-no, garlic fried rice called SI-nan-gag, and a fried egg called it-LOG—give you the dish's name TO-CI-LOG!

2 pounds pork shoulder

⅛ cup dark brown sugar, packed

⅛ cup white sugar

¼ teaspoon kosher salt

1 tablespoon low-sodium soy sauce

¼ cup pineapple juice

2 tablespoons rice wine vinegar or white wine vinegar

1 teaspoon garlic powder

1 teaspoon onion powder

3 garlic cloves, minced

Fried egg, for serving

Fried Rice, for serving (opposite)

In a large bowl, combine the pork shoulder, sugars, salt, soy sauce, pineapple juice, vinegar, garlic powder, onion powder, and fresh garlic. Massage the pork for about 15 minutes. Marinate, covered in the refrigerator, for 6 to 12 hours.

In a sauté pan, place the pork and fill the pan with water until it's covered. Simmer on medium heat for about 60 minutes, or until the water evaporates and the meat is tender (if not, add another ¼ cup of water).

When tender, adjust the heat to medium-high and cook the pork for about 5 minutes more, or until the pan is glazy (fat from the pork will render out, creating oil that will help fry the meat).

Transfer the pork to a cutting board and let it rest for 5 minutes before slicing.

Transfer the sliced pork to a serving platter and serve with fried egg and fried rice.

Nutrition Tip: If you prefer a marinade that is not sweet, reduce the sugar by half.

FRIED RICE *(the Philippines)*

Serves 6 to 8

Fried rice is something that we all love but can't seem to ever get right. Chef Joel says the secret is to use day-old rice. Now you have a way to upcycle the rice that came with your takeout! Fresh rice is too "fresh" and just doesn't have the dryness that will allow each kernel to separate, giving you that incredible crisp that we all love. This fried rice stands on its own but can be served with other dishes like Tocilog. Feel free to get creative and try the dish with different types of rice and veggies.

2 tablespoons avocado oil, plus more for the pan

3 garlic cloves, crushed with skin

3 large eggs

4 cups cooked white jasmine rice (day-old rice is best!)

½ cup low-sodium soy sauce

1 cup frozen peas and carrots

1 tablespoon minced fresh ginger

2 tablespoons sesame oil

Pinch of MSG

Pinch of flaky sea salt, such as Maldon

Freshly ground black pepper

2 scallions, sliced on a bias, for garnish

Place a large nonstick cast-iron skillet on medium-low heat and add the avocado oil and crushed garlic with skin. Remove the pan from the heat when the garlic starts to brown. Throw out the garlic skin only, keeping the oil and garlic in the pan. Do not clean the pan.

In the same pan on medium heat, scramble the eggs; once set, remove the eggs from the pan and rough chop them.

In a separate large bowl, mix the day-old rice with the soy sauce and ¼ cup of water, making sure there are no clumps.

Put the same pan on high heat and add the oil from the garlic bowl . Add the rice and stir for 4 minutes to slightly toast it.

Add the peas and carrots, egg, ginger, sesame oil, MSG, flaky salt, and pepper and cook over high heat for 6 minutes, stirring constantly.

Spoon the fried rice into a bowl and garnish with the scallions.

Ingredient Highlight: Black pepper is used in many dishes and is an unsung powerhouse when it comes to nutrition. It's a great source of antioxidants, particularly piperine, while having anti-inflammatory properties and enhancing the bioavailability and absorption of nutrients found in certain plants.

MAYI MOULIN *(Haiti)*
(CORNMEAL PORRIDGE) WITH SMOKED HERRING

Nothing says breakfast like cornmeal porridge. Mayi moulin *is typically served with* sos pwa nwa, *a black bean sauce. This vegetable-forward version highlights the umami flavor of mineral-rich smoked herring alongside sweet tomatoes. It's a nutrient-dense hearty breakfast that comes together quickly.*

2 tablespoons olive oil

1 Roma tomato, diced

¼ cup diced sweet yellow onion

2 garlic cloves, minced

1 tablespoon tomato paste

2 cups coarse cornmeal, rinsed

1 sprig fresh thyme

2 sprigs fresh flat-leaf parsley

1 (6.7-ounce) can natural smoked wild kippers or herring, skin removed and broken into 1-inch pieces

7 to 8 cups low-sodium chicken broth

Kosher salt and freshly ground black pepper to taste

1 avocado, peeled, pitted, and sliced (optional)

Pikliz (page 137), for garnish

In a large heavy-bottomed pot or Dutch oven, heat the oil over medium-high heat.

Add the tomato and onion and cook for 3 to 5 minutes, until the onions start to brown. Add the garlic and tomato paste and cook for 1 to 2 minutes more, making sure not to burn the garlic.

Add the cornmeal, thyme, parsley, fish, and 4 cups of the broth. Bring just to a boil, then reduce to a simmer and cover.

Check back frequently, every 8 to 10 minutes, to stir and add more chicken stock when needed. Continue in this fashion for 60 to 70 minutes, until the cornmeal is soft but still has some texture. Season with salt and pepper.

To serve, ladle the porridge into bowls and serve with sliced avocado (if using) and pikliz.

Nutrition Tip: Coarse ground cornmeal is a whole grain because the germ and bran have not been removed. It's higher in fiber than a hominy, which has had the outer hulls removed.

KAO DTOM KOONG *(Thailand)*

(RICE PORRIDGE)

Savory nourishing breakfasts are a staple in Thailand. If you travel throughout the country, you may find many versions of this breakfast porridge, sometimes made with pork, and every person will have their preferred way of finishing the dish. This version highlights shrimp and ginger, both loved for their flavor as well as nutrient profiles. I encourage you to get creative with the fresh herbs and spices.

3 cups low-sodium chicken stock

2 cups cooked jasmine rice

½ pound jumbo-size shrimp, cleaned, peeled, and deveined

¼ cup fresh ginger, peeled and chopped

1 tablespoon fish sauce

1 teaspoon white pepper

1 sprig cilantro, finely chopped

In a medium saucepan over medium-high heat, bring the chicken stock to a boil.

Once boiling, add the rice, shrimp, and 1 tablespoon of the ginger. Stirring often, let it cook for about 5 minutes, or until the shrimp is thoroughly cooked.

Season with the fish sauce and turn off the heat.

To serve, transfer the rice into a bowl. Garnish with the white pepper, cilantro, and the remaining ginger.

Prep Tip: You can make the rice in advance and store it in the refrigerator for up to 5 days. That way, the porridge will be ready in minutes.

Ingredient Highlight: The use of ginger for antioxidant and anti-nausea properties has been widely studied in scientific literature. The bioactive compounds found in ginger have the ability to reduce the development of chronic disease and inflammation by reducing reactive oxygen species in the body. Ginger has also long been used for its anti-nausea properties, being shown as effective in pregnancy-induced nausea and vomiting as well as motion sickness.

According to Chef Hong, some Thai people prefer adding extra fried garlic onto the rice porridge and seasoning with chili, vinegar, and fish sauce.

The subcontinent of India houses one of the most diverse societies in the world. With a huge multitude of regional and cultural influences, interwoven with caste, religion, and heritage, the complexities of Indian cuisine can be attributed to the incorporation of flavors and culinary techniques from the societies that have shaped India's history.

Central Asian invaders formed several dynasties from the twelfth to the sixteenth centuries, followed by the Mughal dynasty from the sixteenth to the nineteenth century. The British East India Company came to India to trade and stayed in power from 1757 to 1858, then the British Crown assumed rule as the British Raj from 1858 to 1947. These invaders brought with them new ingredients such as dried fruits and leavened wheat breads as well as preparation techniques such as cooking meat on skewers in the tandoor.

British and other Western powers such as Portugal ventured to India in search of spices and dominance. They brought along potatoes, tomatoes, and chilies, which are now an integral part of Indian cuisine. The food system encourages in-season consumption due to the vast geography and climate. Influences from neighboring countries have an effect on regional staples. South India shares similarities with China and other nearby Asian countries, focusing on rice, vegetables, and seafood, while Northern India's staple grain is wheat and the eating pattern is reliant on meat and dairy products.

GOLDEN OATMEAL *(India)*

Morning oats are an incredibly nourishing way to start the day, especially when paired with antioxidant-rich turmeric and black pepper. This savory version uses jaggery, an unrefined sugar, as the sweetener and boasts a beautiful yellow-orange color. If you are short on time, you can batch prepare and reheat it as needed.

1 cup plain unsweetened oat milk

Pinch of kosher salt

1 cup rolled oats

1 teaspoon jaggery

2 teaspoons ground turmeric

Pinch of freshly ground black pepper

2 whole cardamom pods

2 tablespoons non-hydrogenated plant-based spread

½ cup blueberries, for garnish

½ cup raspberries, for garnish

Ingredient Highlight: Cardamom is an excellent source of potassium as well as other vitamins and trace minerals. It has some antioxidant properties and may aid in digestion.

In a medium pot over high heat, bring 1 cup of water and the oat milk and salt to a boil. Once boiling, add the oats, stir, and reduce the heat to medium-low. Add the jaggery, turmeric, black pepper, and cardamom pods. Stir and continue simmering for 6 to 8 minutes, until the oats have swelled and are soft and the oatmeal is bright yellow.

Add 1 tablespoon of the non-hydrogenated plant-based spread and stir. Pour the oatmeal into a bowl and garnish with the berries and remaining tablespoon of non-hydrogenated plant-based spread. Serve immediately. Enjoy!

# MÜESLI *(Switzerland)*

My first trip to Switzerland with my boyfriend, who would later become my husband, was one to remember. It was during the Christmas season, filled with all of the holiday magic. We traveled to Flims, and I remember his mother made a huge *batch of* bircher müesli *that was bursting with taste and texture from the oats, nuts, and seeds. This was one of many hearty, tummy-warming meals, and each one was better than the last.*

¼ cup wheat germ

2 cups rolled oats

½ cup sliced almonds

½ cup walnuts

½ cup pumpkin seeds

¼ cup ground flaxseeds

½ cup dried blueberries, no added sugar

4 cups plain whole-milk yogurt

1 medium apple, grated

⅓ cup 100% orange juice

Ingredient Highlight: Oats are packed with fiber, specifically beta-glucans. Not only do oats help keep blood sugars level, but they are also a powerful aid when it comes to reducing total cholesterol.

In a large bowl, mix the wheat germ, oats, almonds, walnuts, pumpkin seeds, flaxseeds, and dried blueberries. Add the yogurt, apple, and orange juice then mix to combine. Place the bowl in the refrigerator for 30 minutes.

Spoon into a bowl and enjoy!

Swiss cuisine is defined as much by the countries with which it shares borders and languages as it is by Switzerland itself. There are twenty full cantons or states in **Switzerland**, each unique in its own way. Some are bilingual where people speak both French and German, and others are trilingual with people speaking Romansh, German, and Italian. And many of the German-speaking Swiss speak the native dialect of Swiss-German, which can be heard daily in my home.

French-speaking Switzerland most notably produces Gruyère cheese, *longeole* pork sausage, *saucisson vaudois*, and *damassine*. Ticino, the Italian-speaking region, is famous for its osso bucco, polenta, and minestrone soup, which are all heavily influenced by the Italian neighbors to the south. In the Graubünden region, which borders Liechtenstein, specialties include *bündnerfleisch*, walnut cake, and barley soup; while in German-speaking Switzerland, *spätzli* and *läckerli* biscuits are commonly found throughout the year.

PAN CON TOMATE *(Spain)*

(BREAD WITH TOMATOES)

Vitamin-rich tomatoes—specifically ripe, sweet, and juicy tomatoes—are the star of this dish. The simple ingredients allow the acidity and sweetness of tomatoes to dance together and delight your taste buds. Tomato season is generally May through October in North America; however, this can vary depending on where you live. Try to source in-season tomatoes for the best flavor.

6 slices whole wheat sourdough bread

3 fresh spring garlic cloves

10 ripe red plum tomatoes

Kosher salt and freshly ground black pepper to taste

Extra-virgin olive oil (cold pressed) to taste, plus more for garnish

Dried oregano, for garnish

Fresh chorizo, cooked and crumbled, for garnish (optional)

Ingredient Highlight: Sourdough bread is made with a fermented mother, a naturally occurring yeast made from flour and water, in place of commercial baker's yeast. Sourdough tends to be rich in prebiotic fibers that are beneficial for digestion and gut health.

Preheat the oven to 400°F. Toast the bread in the oven for 5 minutes, remove, and rub the garlic directly on the bread and set aside.

With a box grater, finely grate the tomatoes. In a medium mixing bowl, add the tomato liquid and pulp, then season with the salt, black pepper, and extra-virgin olive oil.

To serve, top the garlic bread with the tomato mixture, garnish with oregano and chorizo (if using), and enjoy.

The Mediterranean triad of grains, grapevines, and olives underpins bread, wine, and olive oil—the staples of many Spanish meals. Indeed, **Spain** has been the world's leading olive oil–producing nation for several years, accounting for more than 40 percent of global production.

Spain's cuisine is also heavily influenced by the Byzantine and Moorish eras in the Middle Ages. During these times, advanced irrigation technologies were developed as were new culinary techniques such as *escabeche*, in which marinated meat or fish is lightly cooked in an acid-based sauce. Entering the modern era, the exchange of plants, animals, culture, and ideas between the Americas and Europe strongly influenced Spanish cuisine. Suddenly, tomatoes, potatoes, maize, and bell peppers were available throughout Spain and the rest of Europe. Culinary staples such as tortilla de patata, Gazpacho de Tomate (page 97), and Pan con Tomate (at left) began to evolve into their current forms.

SEEDED CRACKER

(Scandinavia)

This cracker is so simple to put together you'll never purchase a store-bought seeded cracker again. Packed with plant-based protein and omega-3 fatty acids from the seeds as well as the most scrumptious spices, this cracker makes the perfect pairing for Gravlax (page 175) or any topping of your choice. This recipe calls for onion and chives, but you could easily add garlic or another spice if that sounds delicious to you.

2 cups sunflower seeds

¾ cup hulled hempseeds

2 cups chia seeds

4 cups pumpkin seeds

¼ cup sesame seeds

¾ cup flaxseeds

¼ teaspoon kosher salt

2 tablespoons dried chives

½ teaspoon onion powder

½ teaspoon freshly ground black pepper

Ingredient Highlight: Fiber alert! All of the seeds in this recipe are rich sources of fiber that support digestive health, slow down the absorption of sugar into the bloodstream, and support healthy blood lipid levels.

Preheat the oven to 350°F. Line a sheet pan with parchment paper and set aside.

In a medium bowl, combine all the ingredients and 1⅔ cups of water. Set it aside to rest for 15 minutes.

Evenly spread the mixture over the sheet pan and bake for 30 minutes. Rotate the sheet pan and bake for another 30 minutes, until the crackers are crispy.

Remove the pan from the oven and allow to cool.

To serve, break up the crackers into uneven shapes and store in an airtight container for up to 10 days.

KIND OF *(Greece)*
KOULOURAKIA
(EASTER COOKIES)

Koulourakia, *a type of cookie, are traditionally made in Greece around Easter and loved for their signature buttery and sweet flavor. This version is a bit more savory with a hint of spice due to the use of a variety of flours— including einkorn and whole wheat. Savory cookies are delicious with an excellent cup of coffee or tea or paired with creamy plain yogurt.*

2 cups all-purpose einkorn flour

1 cup all-purpose flour, plus more for rolling the dough

1 cup whole wheat flour

1½ teaspoons baking powder

Zest of 2 oranges

½ cup honey

½ cup unsalted non-hydrogenated plant-based butter, at room temperature

2 large eggs, at room temperature

1 large egg yolk, at room temperature

½ cup oat milk, at room temperature

2 teaspoons ouzo

2 teaspoons ground star anise

2 tablespoons black and white sesame seeds, for sprinkling

Ingredient Highlight: Ouzo is a Greek liqueur distilled from grapes and flavored with anise. Some say it has a hint of licorice and absinthe.

Preheat the oven to 375°F. Place the rack in the center of the oven. Line a sheet pan with parchment paper.

Sift together the flours and baking powder and set aside.

In the bowl of a stand mixer fitted with the paddle attachment, whisk together the orange zest, honey, and butter for about 5 minutes, or until creamy. Then add the eggs and egg yolk one at a time, while the mixer continues running.

Add the oat milk, ouzo, and star anise. Beat together for 30 seconds.

On low speed, add the flour mixture. The dough should not stick to your hands but should be soft. If necessary, add the flour 1 tablespoon at a time.

Remove the dough from the bowl and roll into a ball. Then on a lightly floured surface, roll the dough into a 12-inch log and cut into ½-inch circles—or use your favorite cookie-cutter shape.

Line a sheet pan with parchment paper. Place cookie-dough circles onto the parchment paper about 1 inch apart. Brush the tops with 1 tablespoon of water and sprinkle with the sesame seeds. Bake for 10 to 13 minutes, until the cookies are golden brown. Transfer the cookies to a wire rack and allow to cool.

Enjoy the cookies with your favorite beverage and a friend!

Nutrition Tip: If you are thinking about your blood sugars, you can substitute date syrup for the honey and increase the amount of whole wheat flour used. These swaps will have a lower glycemic index and produce a slower blood sugar spike.

GREECE

Greece is one of the oldest civilizations on record. And its food culture has equally ancient roots, with evidence dating back to 6000 to 4000 BCE of the cereals, legumes, and vegetables that remain the cornerstones of Greek patterns of eating today. Historically, trade has been an integral part of Greek expansion and development. The country's location along the Mediterranean made way for culinary influences from Africa, Asia, and the Middle East. Moussaka, a dish made with eggplant, is said to have arrived in Greece via Turkey with Arab and European influence. Olives, figs, and other vine-based fruits may have arrived later and remain in the region to this day.

The traditional Greek eating pattern has always been rich in plants with some animal foods as well. Frequently consumed foods include stews and salads teeming with vegetables such as zucchini, eggplant, cabbage leaves, and grape leaves. Grains such as rice and bulgur are commonplace, as are herbs such as dill, parsley, coriander, and oregano. Fermented dairy from sheep and goats provides high-quality protein. Meat and chicken are traditionally consumed as the accompaniment rather than the center of the plate. And perhaps most notably, olive oil always has a central place at the table.

CIAMBELLONE (Italy)

(BUNDT CAKE) WITH ROASTED GRAPES

This recipe was shared with me by my dear friend Chef Silvia Barban. She told me that the cake was reminiscent of her childhood in Italy, which was filled with movement and play. The recipe originally called for figs and was inspired by her grandmother's best friend, Signora Rosa, who had a fantastic fig tree and made this cake only when the fig tree was fruiting. To mimic the deep flavor of figs, we cooked the grapes in maple sugar.

For the cake

4 large eggs, at room temperature

¾ cup maple sugar

½ cup almond milk, no added sugar

2¾ cups whole wheat pastry flour, plus more for dusting

1 tablespoon baking powder

½ cup extra-virgin olive oil

Juice and zest of 1 orange

Cooking spray for greasing a Bundt pan

For the sauce

2 tablespoons maple sugar

2 bunches red seedless grapes

2 sprigs fresh mint

Juice and zest of 2 lemons

6 fresh figs, cut in half

Make the cake: Preheat the oven to 320°F.

In a large mixing bowl, whisk together the eggs and sugar with a hand mixer for 10 minutes, until the volume of the eggs doubles in size. Stir in the almond milk.

In a medium bowl, combine the flour and baking powder, then gradually sift into the egg mixture while stirring with a rubber spatula, folding from bottom to top. Fold in the olive oil and orange juice and zest and set aside.

Meanwhile, spray a Bundt pan with the cooking spray and dust lightly with flour. Pour the mixture into the Bundt pan and bake for 30 minutes.

Make the sauce: In a medium saucepan over medium-low heat, place the sugar and cook for about 4 minutes, or until caramelized, taking care not to burn the sugar. Add the grapes, mint leaves from 1 sprig, lemon juice and zest, figs, and ½ cup of water and cook for 5 to 6 minutes, allowing the mixture to thicken and the grapes to blister.

To serve, slice the cake and top each slice with a spoonful of grapes, figs, and sauce, and garnish with the remaining mint leaves.

Ingredient Highlight: Figs are a nutrient-rich fruit that are an excellent source of fiber. There is some compelling research focused on their beneficial role in vascular and heart health.

SOUPS, CURRIES & STEWS

2

CAJUN GUMBO *(American South)*

Cajun food is native to the bayous of New Orleans, influenced by French Canadian and British colonization and richly flavored by a mix of African and Indigenous traditions. This particular version gets much of its depth from the roux, so be sure to take the time to cook it and allow the depth of flavor to develop. The assortment of well-cooked vegetables adds a bite that your taste buds will love.

¼ cup avocado oil

1 pound low-sodium Andouille sausage, sliced in ½-inch pieces

½ cup whole wheat flour

4 tablespoons (½ stick) unsalted butter

½ cup diced celery

1 cup diced yellow onion

¼ cup scallions, white and light green parts chopped

1 red bell pepper, diced

3 garlic cloves, minced

4 cups low-sodium chicken stock

2 cups shredded rotisserie chicken

1½ cups fresh okra, sliced in ½-inch pieces

2 tablespoons Cajun seasoning

1 bay leaf

2 tablespoons Louisiana-style hot sauce

1 pound raw jumbo shrimp, peeled and deveined

¼ cup chopped fresh parsley

Freshly ground black pepper

Rice, for serving

In a large heavy-bottomed pot over medium-high heat, add the oil. Add the sausage and cook about 3 minutes, or until browned.

Remove the sausage from the pot and set aside. There will be oil and browned bits remaining in the pot. Reduce the heat to medium-low and add the flour and butter. Stir frequently, 10 to 15 minutes, until the roux is deep golden brown (but not burned).

Add the celery, onion, scallions, bell pepper, and garlic and continue to cook for 5 minutes more. Add the chicken stock, reserved sausage, chicken, okra, Cajun seasoning, bay leaf, and hot sauce. Increase the temperature to medium-high until the soup begins to simmer, then reduce the temperature to medium-low and cover. Cook for 50 to 60 minutes.

Add the shrimp and parsley, increase the temperature to medium, and cook for 7 minutes. Season with a generous amount of freshly ground pepper.

To serve, spoon the gumbo, without a bay leaf, into a bowl over rice of your choice.

Nutrition Tip: You'll notice that this recipe calls for low-sodium sausage and chicken stock and does not call for additional salt. The sodium from these foods is sufficient; therefore, additional salt is not required. This also allows the flavors from the vegetables and animal proteins to shine.

Ingredient Highlight: Parsley is a powerhouse herb! Half a cup provides more than 500 percent of the recommended daily intake of vitamin K, which is crucial for proper blood clotting and bone health.

ARIMA-STYLE CURRY SHRIMP

(Trinidad and Tobago)

As you travel the globe, curry will make many appearances, each time in an interesting and tasty variation. This particular curry gets its flavor from a mixture of earthy spices that are rich in bioactive components that have anti-inflammatory capacity. The use of herbs and spices reduces the need for added salts, making this curry a heart-healthy option.

3 tablespoons avocado oil

3 sprigs thyme

3 garlic cloves, smashed

3 tablespoons Tagarigua-Style Curry Powder (opposite)

¼ cup full-fat coconut milk

1 pound shrimp (26 to 30 count)

1 tomato, diced

1 medium yellow onion, coarsely chopped

2 celery stalks, coarsely chopped

Roti skin or rice, for serving

In a large Dutch oven or other heavy-bottomed pot over low heat, heat the oil.

Add the thyme, garlic, and curry powder and cook, stirring frequently until aromatic, taking care not to burn the curry.

Add the coconut milk and cook for 3 minutes. Add the shrimp and cook for 2 to 3 more minutes. Add the tomato and ¼ cup of water.

Finally, add the onion and celery and cook for 20 minutes, adding water, ¼ cup at a time as needed. Make sure the liquid has been absorbed, depending on the size of the shrimp.

To serve, spoon the curry on to a plate and enjoy with a roti skin or rice.

Curry in **Trinidad** is heavily influenced by South Asian flavors that transformed as countries were colonized. In the mid-1800s, East Indian people were brought to Trinidad and Tobago as indentured servants. With this migration came an influx of new flavors that were married with African and Indigenous Amerindian flavors.

TAGARIGUA-STYLE CURRY POWDER

(Trinidad and Tobago)

Makes 1 small jar

Curry powder is so simple to make. This one gets its name from the town in Trinidad where my grandmother lived. It's phytonutrient rich and packed with flavor. And once you make this version, you will be confident enough to create your own variations.

Place all the ingredients in a mason jar, cover, and shake vigorously until well combined.

Store in a cool dark place for up to 1 year.

1 tablespoon ground turmeric

1½ teaspoons smoked paprika

1½ teaspoons ground ginger

1½ teaspoons ground cumin

1½ teaspoons ground coriander

¾ teaspoon fennel seeds

1½ teaspoons ground fenugreek

½ teaspoon black mustard seeds

½ teaspoon ground mace

½ teaspoon freshly ground black pepper

Ingredient Highlight: This curry powder is a combination of many different spices including turmeric, fenugreek, coriander, and cumin. Each of these spices has an excellent nutritional profile, all boasting anti-inflammatory, anticancer, and antioxidant effects. Adding some black pepper to your dish can help increase the absorption of curcumin, the bioactive compound found in turmeric.

BRANZINO *(France)*
BOUILLABAISSE
(FISH STEW)

Before becoming the "it" stew, bouillabaisse was the kitchen sink of seafood stews, utilizing less expensive fish and shellfish. Overflowing with fiber-rich vegetables and an abundance of seafood, this stew deserves its place in the spotlight. Today, shellfish has been elevated in status from pauper to royalty, and bouillabaisse is fit for a dinner party. Make this in advance of a large gathering, and allow the flavors to come together even more for a better-than-yesterday taste.

1 large bulb of fennel, diced, fronds reserved

2 cups diced celery

2 medium yellow onions, coarsely chopped

1 large carrot, coarsely chopped

6 fresh bay leaves

½ cup extra-virgin olive oil

1 cup dry white wine

1 bunch fresh thyme

4 wild anchovies

Ingredient Highlight: Saffron, the most expensive spice in the world, is the gold of the spice pantry. It takes 75,000 saffron flowers to make 1 pound of saffron spice.

2 whole branzino, cleaned and cut into quarters

½ cup rye flour, for dusting

5 large Yukon Gold potatoes, washed and diced with the skin on

2 teaspoons ground cayenne pepper

1 tablespoon saffron

1 cup vermouth

6 cups fish broth

1 heirloom tomato, coarsely chopped

1 pound mussels, cleaned

1 pound tail-on shrimp, cleaned

1 pound scallops, cleaned (be sure to remove the foot of the scallops)

1 teaspoon freshly ground black pepper, plus more as needed

1 teaspoon red pepper flakes

Juice of 1 large lemon

Kosher salt

Crusty bread, for serving

In a 9-quart stockpot over medium heat, place the fennel, celery, onions, carrot, bay leaves, and ¼ cup of the olive oil and cook for 15 minutes, until all the vegetables are tender. Add the white wine, thyme, and anchovies and bring to a simmer, reducing until there is no liquid, about 15 minutes.

Meanwhile, dust the branzino with rye flour and set aside. Heat a 9-inch cast-iron skillet over medium-high heat, add the remaining ¼ cup olive oil and the dusted fish, and fry 5 to 7 minutes, until golden brown on each side, then remove from the pan and set aside.

Recipe continues

Add the potatoes to the same skillet and cook for 6 minutes, stirring often, until golden on all sides. Add the cayenne and saffron and stir. Turn the heat off and add the vermouth to deglaze the potatoes. Turn the heat back to medium and cook the potatoes for 5 more minutes. Add the fish broth and tomato, then cook for 15 minutes.

Carefully remove a quarter of the potato mixture from the heat and place into a blender. Pour the remaining mixture through a sieve into the stockpot filled with veggies, reserving the cooked potato and tomato. Add the reserved potato and tomato to the blender and blend until smooth. Return the blended mixture to the stockpot and add 2 cups of water.

Bring the soup to a simmer and add the mussels, shrimp, scallops, fish, fennel fronds, black pepper, red pepper flakes, and lemon juice and cook about 6 minutes, or until the mussels open.

Season with salt and pepper to taste.

To serve, ladle a heaping portion of the soup, being sure to get all the ingredients except the bay leaf, into a deep soup bowl. Enjoy with a fresh piece of crusty bread.

BERBERE-SPICED CHICKPEA STEW

WITH POACHED EGGS

Chef Gerald, who contributed this recipe, reminisced that this particular stew is inspired by fragrant Moroccan spice markets. Depending on the time of year, temperatures can oscillate from cool and wet to warm and dry. Heavy on the vegetables and spices and low on the salt, this tomato-rich stew has a clay color evocative of the rich red soils of the region.

¼ cup avocado oil

1 cup diced yellow onion

½ cup diced carrots

½ cup diced celery

1 garlic clove, thinly sliced

6 tablespoons tomato paste

5 tablespoons berbere spice

1 (15-ounce) can low-sodium chickpeas, drained and rinsed

3 cups low-sodium chicken broth

Kosher salt

6 large eggs

1 cup plain whole-milk yogurt

1 English cucumber, thinly sliced

1 slice sourdough bread per person

1 bunch chives, chopped, for garnish

12 sprigs fresh mint, torn, for garnish (2 sprigs per person)

Preheat the oven to 400°F.

In a large cast-iron skillet, add the oil, onion, carrot, and celery and cook over medium-high heat until translucent. Add the garlic and cook until tender.

Add the tomato paste. Caramelize with the vegetables until well-toasted. Add the berbere and toast for 1 minute more.

Add the chickpeas and broth. Cook over medium heat until the liquid is reduced and a thick stew forms. Season the stew with salt to taste.

Crack the eggs into the stew, evenly distributed. Cover and place the stew in the oven. Bake 12 to 18 minutes, until the eggs set.

Meanwhile, mix the yogurt and cucumber in a small bowl and toast the sourdough.

Serve by placing the skillet on the table to enjoy family-style, with toast on the side. Garnish with chives and mint.

Ingredient Highlight: Berbere is a spice hailing from Ethiopia that is based upon chilies. These hot chilies contain capsaicin, an antioxidant compound that can support healthy blood-sugar levels and may reduce the symptoms and incidence of metabolic syndrome.

ITAL STEW *(Jamaica)*

Rastafarianism is a faith-based movement steeped in politics and encompasses much more than the stereotype of people with dreadlocks who listen to reggae. Ital is the core of the whole foods–based vegetarian eating patterns that Rastafarians follow. Ital food is said to contain the vital and beneficial essence of plants. This Ital stew is literally loaded with a variety of nutrient-rich plants.

1 yellow onion, diced

2 scallions (white and green parts), thinly chopped

3 cloves garlic, thinly sliced

2 teaspoons avocado oil

3 sprigs fresh thyme

4 bay leaves

1 (15-ounce) can full-fat coconut milk

5 cups low-sodium vegetable broth

2 cups pumpkin, cut into 2-inch cubes

½ cup split peas

1 ear of corn, cut lengthwise into 2-inch pieces

2 green plantains, cut into 2-inch pieces

2 Roma tomatoes, coarsely chopped

1 teaspoon kosher salt

Juice and zest of 2 lemons

1 cup okra, cut into 2-inch pieces

1 habanero pepper

Lime wedges, for garnish

1 bunch fresh cilantro, torn, for garnish

In a large heavy-bottomed pot over medium heat, place the onion, scallions, garlic, and oil. Cook for 3 to 5 minutes, stirring occasionally and taking care not to burn the garlic. Add 1 cup of water and cook for an additional 5 minutes.

Add the thyme, bay leaves, coconut milk, broth, pumpkin, and split peas, and cook uncovered over medium-high heat for 8 minutes. Next, add the corn, plantains, tomatoes, salt, and lemon juice and zest, and cook for 30 minutes.

Add the okra and habanero and cook for 15 to 20 minutes.

To serve, spoon the stew into a bowl and garnish with a wedge of lime and fresh cilantro.

HARIRA *(Middle East + North Africa)*

WITH CAULIFLOWER AND COUSCOUS

Harira is a classic Moroccan soup made from an assortment of vegetables and chickpeas. In this version, the tangy yet sweet flavor of apricots pairs with the earthy warmth of cinnamon and simmers with the spice from the chermoula, *making for a rich and hearty soup. You can batch prepare this soup in advance and enjoy it for days.*

4 fresh bay leaves, or 6 dry bay leaves

1 bunch cilantro, stems and leaves separated

2 teaspoons ground coriander

4 cinnamon sticks

5 ounces coarsely chopped dry apricot

3 tablespoons extra-virgin olive oil

1 cup chermoula

1 red onion, coarsely chopped

1 head cauliflower, coarsely chopped

1 (15-ounce) can low-sodium chickpeas

1 carrot, coarsely chopped

4 Roma tomatoes, coarsely chopped into 2-inch chunks

6 cups low-sodium vegetable broth

1 teaspoon kosher salt

Juice of 1 lemon

2 cups dry barley couscous, cooked, for serving

Lemon wedges, for serving

Ingredient Highlight: Chermoula is a combination of herbs, spices, and vegetables that is packed with fiber to support gut health. It can be purchased online.

In a 9-quart Dutch oven or large stockpot over medium heat, place the bay leaves, cilantro stems, coriander, cinnamon, apricot, and olive oil and cook for 2 minutes, stirring often. The spices will be fragrant.

Add the chermoula, onion, cauliflower, chickpeas, carrot, and tomatoes and cook for 3 minutes. Add the vegetable broth and salt, cover, and bring to a boil, about 8 minutes. Then reduce to medium heat and cook for 40 minutes.

Add the lemon juice and mix. To serve, ladle the soup into a bowl and enjoy with a spoonful of couscous and lemon wedge.

The intersection of religion and politics has shaped North African foodways, as have topography and climate. Religious customs and law define a significant portion of culinary culture as the majority of the people living in **North Africa** are Muslims. Pork and alcohol are often omitted from meals, and culinary flavors are influenced by neighboring African, Middle Eastern, and other Mediterranean nations. Coriander, cumin, and fennel are common spices. Date, olive, and almond trees as well as grapevines are able to grow in the arid climate, and they feature heavily in the cuisine. Durable crops such as hard wheat and sorghum form the basis for staple dishes such as couscous, bulgur, and breads. Across the region, traditional breads with roots in the Ottoman Empire are made using hard wheat.

Storage Tip: This soup can be stored in an airtight container in the refrigerator for up to 5 days. Or place it in a freezer-safe container and freeze for up to 3 months.

LEGUME *(Haiti)*

(STEWED VEGETABLES) WITH DUNGENESS CRAB

Depending on the Haitian kitchen you walk into, legume will be prepared differently. This dish packs in an abundance of diverse vegetables with varying nutrient profiles. The veggies are stewed down, resulting in a softer texture, and as the dish cooks, the flavors become even deeper. The addition of the crab imparts a hint of the sea and will have you licking your fingers and sucking on the shells!

2 tablespoons olive oil

½ medium white onion, diced

2 scallions (white and light green parts), chopped

2 garlic cloves, minced

3 Roma tomatoes, diced

3 chayote squash, chopped

2 medium carrots, chopped

2 medium eggplants, chopped

½ head cabbage, cut in large pieces

1 cup chopped spinach

1 cup chopped watercress

½ red or orange bell pepper, diced

3 sprigs fresh thyme

2 tablespoons chopped fresh parsley

1 teaspoon vegetable bouillon, such as Better Than Bouillon

3 Dungeness crabs, cleaned and quartered

Kosher salt and freshly ground black pepper

White rice, for serving

Pikliz (page 137), for serving

In a large pot over medium-high heat, heat the olive oil. Add the onion, scallions, and garlic and sauté for 3 minutes. Add the tomatoes and cook for 5 minutes.

Add the squash, carrots, and eggplant. Cover and reduce heat to medium. Cook for 5 minutes, until the veggies start to sweat. Stir and continue to cook for 10 minutes more.

Add the cabbage, spinach, watercress, bell pepper, thyme, parsley, vegetable bouillon, and crabs, as well as 1½ cups of water. Cover and cook for 35 to 45 minutes, until the vegetables are very soft and combined. If the legumes reduce too quickly, add more water ½ cup at a time. Season with salt and pepper.

To serve, transfer the legumes and one-quarter of the cooked crab to a large serving bowl and enjoy with white rice and pikliz.

Nutrition Tip: This recipe is packed with fiber! Specifically soluble fiber that helps to slow down the absorption of sugar and to support healthy blood sugar and lipid levels.

Substitution Tip: If you are not able to find Dungeness crab, you can use 1 pound crabmeat.

ST. ELIZABETH *(Jamaica)*
VEGETABLE CURRIED CHICKPEAS

Serves 8 to 10

For the majority of my teen years, my family would spend extended time over summer breaks in Treasure Beach, St. Elizabeth Parish, Jamaica, at a wonderful place called Ital Rest. It was a natural paradise by the ocean, filled with fruit trees, a place where I made strong friendships. To me, Ital Rest was the jewel of St. Elizabeth. All of our meals were vegetarian, like this vegetarian curry, as the property owners were Rastafarian and requested that no meat be prepared on the premises. It was on these trips that I was introduced to new flavors and Jamaican culture.

¼ cup coconut oil

5 garlic cloves, minced

4 tablespoons minced fresh ginger

1 medium onion, thinly sliced

½ cup Jamaican curry powder

6 cups mushroom stock

Juice of 1 lime

6 sprigs fresh thyme

6 sprigs fresh cilantro

3 scallions (white and light green parts), chopped

6 bay leaves

1 Scotch bonnet pepper

1 tablespoon kosher salt, plus more as needed

3 to 4 medium russet potatoes, peeled and cut into medium chunks

2 large carrots, diced

Freshly ground black pepper

White rice or peas and rice, for serving

In a 9-quart Dutch oven or large stockpot over medium-high heat, heat the oil. Add the garlic, ginger, and onion and cook for 5 to 7 minutes. Add the curry powder and cook for 5 more minutes.

Add 4 cups of the mushroom stock, as well as the lime juice, thyme, cilantro, scallions, bay leaves, Scotch bonnet pepper, and salt. Bring to a simmer.

Add the potatoes and carrots to the Dutch oven and stir to combine. Reduce the heat to low, cover tightly, and simmer for 25 to 35 minutes, until the potatoes are soft. If the vegetables have absorbed too much liquid, add 1 to 2 cups of the reserved mushroom stock and simmer for 5 to 7 minutes more. Season with salt and pepper.

To serve, enjoy family-style with white rice or peas and rice.

Substitution Tip: You can swap in low-sodium vegetable broth if you are unable to find mushroom stock.

Nutrition Tip: If you are managing diabetes, you can substitute Carisma, white, or Nicola potatoes for the russet potatoes. Carisma and Nicola potatoes have a lower glycemic index value compared to russet potatoes.

GAZPACHO *(Spain)*
DE TOMATE
(TOMATO SOUP)

Gazpacho is reminiscent of summer and hot balmy days. If you live in New York like I do, hot days bleed into nights when you don't want to turn on the stove, much less cook a labor-intensive meal. Enter gazpacho de tomate, *the perfect accompaniment to grilled fish for the days when you want a simple yet delicious meal that will leave you feeling satisfied and well nourished.*

6 ripe beefsteak or Roma tomatoes, coarsely chopped

1 red onion, coarsely chopped

½ cup sherry vinegar

4 Persian cucumbers, coarsely chopped

¼ teaspoon kosher salt

¼ teaspoon freshly ground black pepper, plus more for garnish

⅓ cup extra-virgin olive oil, plus more for finishing

1 bunch fresh basil, torn, for garnish

1 bunch rainbow radishes, thinly sliced, for garnish

Flaky sea salt, such as Maldon, for garnish

Place the tomato, onion, vinegar, cucumbers, salt, and black pepper in a blender. Blend until smooth. Add the olive oil and pulse until combined.

To serve, spoon the gazpacho into bowls, finish with olive oil, and garnish with basil and radishes. Season with flaky salt and black pepper to taste.

Nutrition Tip: Olive oil is a great source of monounsaturated and polyunsaturated fatty acids, which are known to increase high-density lipoprotein (HDL) or "good" cholesterol. This in turn helps to support cardiovascular health by reducing blood clots, blood pressure, and inflammation. The properties in olive oil may also have some anticarcinogenic properties.

PEANUT *(West and Central Africa)*
MISO STEW

This legume-rich stew provides a great source of plant-based protein as well as vitamins and minerals that support metabolic function and energy production thanks to the peanuts and black-eyed peas. Creamy with a hint of starch, simply delicious. The rich flavors come together in a relatively short amount of time, making it a staple in your rotation.

5 tablespoons no sugar- or salt-added peanut butter

5 tablespoons miso

½ cup diced yellow onion

1 carrot, diced

2 tablespoons avocado oil

½ cup raw peanuts

1 cup cooked black-eyed peas, cooled

5-inch piece of kombu

2 tablespoons honey

Juice and zest of 2 limes

1 tablespoon thinly sliced fresh cilantro

1 tablespoon thinly sliced fresh parsley

1 teaspoon chopped fresh chives

1 jalapeño, sliced thinly into rings, for garnish

2 cups toasted peanuts seasoned with paprika, for garnish

Kosher salt to taste

Mix the peanut butter and miso. Reserve.

In a large stockpot over medium-high heat, sauté the onions and carrots in avocado oil for 5 to 7 minutes, until translucent.

Add the raw peanuts, black-eyed peas, kombu, and honey, as well as 3 cups of water, and bring to a boil. Cook for approximately 10 minutes, or until the liquid is reduced by a third.

Add the peanut-miso mixture and continue cooking for 10 minutes, until thickened.

Add the lime juice and zest, cilantro, parsley, and chives to the hot stew.

To serve, ladle the hot stew into a bowl and garnish with the thinly sliced jalapeño rings, crunchy peanuts, and salt to taste.

Substitution Tip: If you are unable to find raw peanuts, simply omit them from the recipe and rely on the peanut butter and crunchy peanuts for garnish.

Ingredient Highlight: Peanuts, also known as goobers, are a great shelf-stable source of vitamins, minerals, and plant-based proteins.

Peanuts grow on the Ivory Coast, where they are called groundnuts since they grow underground, as well as in the deep South of the United States. This recipe is a celebration of those legumes while also adding the southern black-eyed pea, another ingredient that is connected to the American South and Western Africa.

West Africa is a vast region encompassing urban as well as savanna and forested areas, landscapes that greatly influence the available foods. Northern savanna areas are friendlier to cereal agriculture (sorghum, millet, and maize), while hotter forest areas are more conducive to tubers such as yams, cassava, and plantains. Climate plays a major role in determining the cooking oils and animal foods traditional to the region as well; people in forested areas generally cooked with palm oil, while in the savanna, peanut oil reigned. Sticky spheres of tubers called *fufu* are a common dish, often accompanying stews made from groundnut or palm oil, okra, spice, and some meat or fish.

During the Middle Passage, enslaved West Africans often brought foods from the continent with them as a matter of survival, which contributed to the spread of traditional West African food to America. Transatlantic trade brought chilies, maize, and cassava to the African continent. Meanwhile, British imperialism took flavors from colonies around the globe and deposited them into Western and Central Africa. Palm chop, a West African dish made with palm oil, animal proteins, and vegetables, for example, was influenced by the curry found throughout South Asia.

As trade with other regions increased over the past two millennia, some foods traditionally thought of as West African migrated to Central Africa. Central African eating patterns began to include cassava, peanuts, tomatoes, beans, taro, rice, sorghum, and millet; many of these became staple crops with some replacing the indigenous crops (e.g., the American peanut displacing the Bambara groundnut).

Throughout these changes, however, stews and starches remain the core of the Central African patterns of eating. Stews are usually composed of a few ingredients and then thickened with palm fruit or crushed peanuts; sometimes other thickeners such as crushed seeds or okra may be used. They are then paired with a boiled and pounded starch, such as cassava. Typically, a small piece is torn off and dipped or dunked in the stew before being eaten. Greens are also a core component of Central African cuisine, including leaves from cassava, okra, pumpkin, sorrel, or sweet potato. These greens, along with onion, hot pepper, meat, fish, and oil, are the typical ingredient base for daily stews. Red palm oil is also unique to the region, made from boiling and hand-squeezing fresh palm nuts.

SWEET POTATO AND LEEK SOUP

(West and Central Africa)

Serves 6

WITH CRISPY POTATO SKINS

Inspired by Nigerian yam production, this simple soup boasts complex flavors and a good dose of fat-soluble vitamins along with phytonutrients. It's hard to find yams in America—yams are larger than sweet potatoes and have a rough darker skin—so in this recipe sweet potato is used. Whiskey imparts some herbal and citrusy notes when paired with the chicken stock to deglaze the pan. The entire soup comes together topped with flavorful crispy potato skins.

5 sweet potatoes, peeled and chopped, peels reserved

3 tablespoons avocado oil

2 leeks, chopped

1 yellow onion, chopped

2 tablespoons ground turmeric

½ teaspoon cayenne pepper

½ cup rye whiskey

6 cups low-sodium chicken stock

Kosher salt and freshly ground black pepper

Juice of 2 limes

Zest of 1 lime

3 tablespoons togarashi

1 cup sour cream, for serving

2 cups cooked quinoa, for serving

1 bunch fresh cilantro, chopped, for serving

In a large stainless steel pot, place the sweet potatoes and 2 tablespoons of the oil over high heat and cook for 3 to 5 minutes, allowing the potatoes to caramelize. Add the leeks, onion, turmeric, and cayenne.

Deglaze the pot with the whiskey, add the chicken stock, and cook for 40 minutes at medium-high heat.

Allow the soup to cool, then carefully blend with an immersion blender. Season with salt and black pepper to taste and add lime juice and lime zest.

Preheat the oven to 400°F.

Season the potato skins with the remaining 1 tablespoon of avocado oil. Place the skins on a sheet pan and cook for about 8 minutes, or until crispy. Place the cooked skins in a shallow bowl and season with the togarashi.

To serve, ladle the soup into a bowl with sour cream and quinoa, then garnish with the cilantro and crispy potato skins.

Ingredient Highlight: Togarashi, also known as the Japanese seven-spice powder, is composed of a variety of ingredients depending on local tradition or the preferences of the cook. Traditionally, it contains chili, orange peel, seaweed, ginger, poppy seeds, and sesame seeds. These spices all exert a wide variety of benefits as a source of vitamins and minerals such as B vitamins and vitamins A, D, and E. Seaweed is an excellent vegetarian source of omega-3s.

SWEET CORN CHOWDER

(Central US)

This easy-to-prepare, sweet chowder is packed with fiber and flavor and topped with pickled vegetables for an unexpected twist. Combining starchy potato and cruciferous cauliflower provides a creamy chowder-like texture. The alternate mouthfeel of the potato crisp and pickled onions makes for a tangy yet crispy bite.

For the corn chowder

2 tablespoons (¼ stick) unsalted butter

2 cups freshly shucked corn (about 4 medium ears)

½ cup diced yellow onion

1 garlic clove, minced

4 cups low-sodium vegetable broth

½ teaspoon kosher salt

½ teaspoon garlic powder

1 large russet potato, diced

1 cup diced cauliflower

½ cup diced celery

½ cup half-and-half

Kosher salt and freshly ground white pepper

1 teaspoon finely diced jalapeño, seeds removed

1 teaspoon chopped chives

For the potato crisp

2 medium white potatoes, sliced into ⅛-inch rounds

1 tablespoon of your favorite pesto

For the pickled red onions

1 medium red onion, thinly sliced

1 cup white or Acid League botanically infused vinegar

Make the corn chowder: In a medium saucepan over medium heat, melt the butter and add the corn, onion, and garlic. Sauté over medium heat, stirring occasionally, for 5 minutes, until the onions are translucent. Add the broth, salt, and garlic powder and simmer, uncovered, another 5 minutes.

Transfer the soup to a blender and purée until smooth. Return the soup to the pot and add the potato, cauliflower, and celery. Bring just to a boil, then reduce the temperature to medium-low and simmer for 12 to 17 minutes, until the vegetables are soft.

Add the half-and-half and stir to combine. Season with salt and white pepper.

Note: When blending hot soups, be mindful to not fill the blender more than two-thirds. If necessary, blend in batches.

Make the potato crisp: Preheat the oven to 350°F.

In a medium bowl, combine the sliced potatoes and pesto and mix. Place the coated potatoes on a sheet pan and bake for 10 to 15 minutes, watching the potatoes to make sure they don't burn.

Make the pickled onions: Place the onions into a shallow bowl and cover with vinegar. Set aside for at least 10 minutes.

Divide the soup between bowls and garnish with the diced jalapeño and chives. Serve with 2 to 4 potato crisps and a dollop of pickled onions. This soup is great as a main course or as a smaller portion alongside a sandwich.

Corn is a high-yield crop that is widely grown throughout the midwestern part of the **United States**. Most sweet corn hasn't been genetically modified, which may be top of mind for some.

Nutrition Tip: If the glycemic index of this dish is of concern, you can substitute the large russet potato in the chowder for a Carisma potato or a sweet potato. Carisma potatoes and sweet potatoes have a lower glycemic index value compared to russet potatoes.

Prep Tip: Swap frozen sweet corn for fresh if it's not corn season or you simply can't find delicious fresh corn.

PLANT FORWARD

3

JAMAICAN-STYLE CALLALOO *(Jamaica)*

Not to be confused with its cousin, Trinidadian callaloo, Jamaican callaloo is typically made with chopped callaloo bush, also known as amaranth greens, which can be found from a number of online retailers. Callaloo bush is equally nutrient rich and as delicious as its Trinidadian cousin dasheen bush. If you are unable to find callaloo bush, you can substitute any hearty, large, leafy green of your choice such as Swiss chard or collard greens.

---

8 to 10 stalks callaloo

1 tablespoon coconut oil

½ cup diced onion

2 scallions (white and light green parts), chopped

2 garlic cloves, minced

1 sprig fresh thyme

1 diced Roma tomato

¼ teaspoon smoked paprika

¼ teaspoon ground allspice

Kosher salt and freshly ground black pepper

Remove the stalk from each callaloo leaf. Gently rinse each leaf two or three times to remove any sand or dirt.

Stack the leaves on top of one another, then roll them tightly. Cut the callaloo into 1-inch ribbons (*chiffonade*). You should have about 4 to 5 cups. Set aside.

In a large skillet over medium heat, heat the coconut oil. Add the onion, scallions, and garlic and cook for 3 minutes. Add the callaloo, thyme, tomato, paprika, and allspice and cook for an additional 5 to 7 minutes.

Season with salt and pepper. Remove the skillet from the heat.

To serve, enjoy with eggs, ackee, Bammy (page 47), or *hardo* bread, a Jamaican bread made with hard wheat, that can be found in specialty or online retailers.

Nutrition Tip: Callaloo refers to the leafy dark greens that are native to the Caribbean and are packed with vitamins and minerals. Callaloo is rich with vitamin C, potassium, B vitamins, and vitamin K, all of which support bone health, healthy blood pressure levels, and are preventative against inflammatory diseases.

HEN OF THE WOODS MUSHROOMS

(East Africa)

Serves 4

WITH CONGEE GRITS AND RED-EYE GRAVY

Originally, this recipe was written with spam as the protein in the dish. Spam, a preserved canned meat sometimes used in dishes throughout the African diaspora, signifies preservation, survival, and perseverance—attributes inherited out of necessity. This dish has been reimagined with meaty mushrooms instead—a plant-forward option in its place.

3 hen of the woods mushrooms, cut into 1-inch "steaks"

2 tablespoons olive oil

¼ teaspoon flaky sea salt, such as Maldon

¼ teaspoon freshly ground black pepper

1 cup grits, such as Anson Mills

3 tablespoons minced fresh ginger

4 tablespoons dashi powder

1 tablespoon avocado oil

¼ cup diced onion

1 cup brewed Ethiopian coffee

2 tablespoons honey

1 teaspoon Worcestershire sauce

½ tablespoon non-hydrogenated plant-based spread

Kosher salt

1 sheet Nori, thinly sliced, for garnish

Preheat the oven to 400°F. Line a sheet pan with parchment paper.

Place the mushroom steaks on the prepared sheet pan and coat them in olive oil, salt, and black pepper. Place the pan in the oven and bake for 10 to 15 minutes, until the mushrooms are crunchy but not burnt. Remove from the oven and set aside.

In a medium stockpot, bring 6 cups of water to a boil and slowly add the grits, whisking the entire time.

Add the ginger and dashi powder and continue to whisk. Reduce to a simmer and continue whisking for approximately 30 minutes, or until the grits are tender, and reserve.

In a medium cast-iron skillet over medium heat, add the avocado oil and onion. Cook for 5 to 7 minutes.

Deglaze the pan with the coffee, add the honey, and cook 10 to 12 minutes, until reduced by half. Season with the Worcestershire sauce.

Cool slightly, then add the plant-based butter to emulsify. Season with salt and reserve.

To assemble, spoon the grits onto a plate and place the mushrooms in the center of the grits. Spoon the sauce on top and drizzle around the plate. Garnish with the nori.

Ingredient Highlight: Dashi powder is a combination of steeped kombu, a dried kelp, and *katsuobushi*, a dried and aged tuna. Kombu is a nutritional powerhouse, containing iodine, which is incredibly important for thyroid health.

WATERMELON STEAK *(East Africa)*

WITH FETA AND MINT

It's impossible not to love watermelon. This lovable melon is incredibly hydrating while being a significant source of antioxidants. Marinating the watermelon in hibiscus and beets intensifies the color while adding sweet yet tart notes. Finishing the dish with a hard sear adds a smoky flavor. Be sure to enjoy the finished product warm for the full complement.

---

1 cup dry hibiscus leaves

⅛ cup sugar dissolved in ⅛ cup warm water

2 beets, coarsely chopped

4 tablespoons tamarind

1 watermelon, cut into 1-inch-thick steaks (cut round then halved, leaving rind as "bone")

Juice of 2 lemons

1 (11.3-ounce) jar oil-cured feta cheese

1 cup fresh mint, tightly packed

Flaky sea salt, such as Maldon, to taste

1 cup fresh basil, tightly packed

In a small stockpot, combine the hibiscus, sugar, beets, and tamarind with 4 cups of water and bring to a boil, then cool.

Strain the liquid and set aside.

Place the beets and hibiscus leaves in a blender with ½ cup of water and purée.

Push the purée through a sieve into the liquid that has been set aside.

Place 2 watermelon steaks at a time in a large gallon-size sealable bag and marinate the "steaks" in the liquid for 30 minutes, being careful to not overdress the "bone" (which is the rind).

Drain the liquid out of the bag and place in a small stockpot over medium heat, cook for 20 minutes to reduce by half, and add the lemon juice.

Place the steaks on the grill and cook for 3 minutes on each side. If cooking in batches, keep the already cooked steaks warm.

To serve, cut off the rind and slice the steak lengthwise. Dress with the reduced liquid, season with feta and mint, and garnish with salt and torn basil.

Prep Tip: When cutting a watermelon, slice a piece from the bottom of the melon to create a base. Place the watermelon on the base for more stable slicing.

Ingredient Highlight: Hibiscus leaves have been shown to decrease blood pressure as well as total cholesterol, LDL cholesterol, and triglycerides. Hibiscus leaves contain an abundance of anthocyanins, the phytochemical responsible for the reduction in these biomarkers.

Enslaved Africans brought a variety of seeds with them on the transatlantic crossing to America. These seeds would grow into plants that provided nourishment and sustenance under the harsh conditions they would experience for centuries and become popular foods enjoyed across cultures. Native to northeastern Africa, watermelon eaten by Black people is often stereotyped and may be regarded as somewhat polarizing among Black American families.

PLANT FORWARD

113

GRANNY'S CALLALOO

(Trinidad and Tobago)

My grandmother always made callaloo with dasheen bush, also known as taro. Sometimes she would use a whole crab for a sweet-and-salty flavor. When she would visit us in Massachusetts, she would replicate the dish with frozen spinach in place of dasheen bush. The greens in the dish provide a variety of micronutrients as well as carotenoid antioxidants. I've made my own version with the greens that are available to me by combining Chinese broccoli and kale, which yields an earthy yet spicy callaloo.

2 ham hocks (optional)

⅓ cup avocado oil

⅓ cup diced fresh chives

1 onion, finely diced

2⅓ cups coarsely chopped pumpkin

1 (13.5-ounce) can full-fat coconut milk

1 tablespoon kosher salt

2 cups okra, coarsely chopped

½ bunch Chinese broccoli, stems and florets separated

½ bunch kale, coarsely chopped

1 green bell pepper, coarsely chopped

1 habanero pepper

Pelau, for serving (page 186)

If using the ham hocks, place them in a large bowl covered with water, cover with a dish towel, and soak them overnight. After 8 to 12 hours, discard the water and set the ham hock aside.

In a heavy-bottomed 8-quart pot, add the oil, chives, onion, and ham hocks. Cook over medium heat for 5 minutes, until golden brown.

Add the pumpkin and cook for 3 to 5 minutes. Next, add the coconut milk and salt as well as 13.5 ounces water (use the empty can as your measuring cup), and cook uncovered for 20 minutes.

Add the okra, Chinese broccoli stems, kale, and bell pepper and cook for 15 minutes.

Add the Chinese broccoli florets and habanero pepper. Reduce heat to low, taking care not to burst the pepper, and cook for 5 minutes.

Carefully remove the pepper and ham hocks from the pot. Use an immersion blender to blitz the veggies until they are a thick stew-like consistency.

To serve, spoon the callaloo onto a plate with the pelau.

Ingredient Highlight: Avocado oil is an excellent substitute for butter. This heart-healthy oil is rich in monounsaturated fats and low in saturated fats, a combination that supports a healthy blood-lipid profile.

PAN-FRIED BLACK-EYED PEAS

(American South)

Black-eyed peas made their way to the American South with enslaved Africans and became a meaningful part of the African American culinary traditions that have significantly influenced American foodways. This fiber-forward, pan-fried version of black-eyed peas is full of vegetables and has a distinctly vinegary bite that pairs well with a heaping plate of greens.

---

5 tablespoons olive oil

¼ cup diced carrot

¼ cup diced celery

½ cup diced onion

3 garlic cloves, minced

3 sprigs fresh thyme, leaves removed from sprig

5 sprigs fresh flat-leaf parsley, leaves and stems coarsely chopped

2½ teaspoons ground cumin

1½ teaspoons smoked paprika

5 tablespoons rice vinegar

2 tablespoons vegan Worcestershire sauce

1 pound frozen or dry black-eyed peas, prepared according to package instructions

⅛ teaspoon kosher salt

⅛ teaspoon freshly ground black pepper

Greens of your choice, for serving

In a large heavy-bottomed pot or Dutch oven, heat 3 tablespoons of the oil over medium-high heat. Add the carrot, celery, and onion. Sauté for 10 to 15 minutes, until the onions and celery are soft and translucent.

Add the garlic and cook for 1 to 2 minutes, making sure not to burn the garlic.

Add the thyme, parsley, cumin, paprika, vinegar, and Worcestershire sauce and stir well. Add the peas, salt, pepper, and the remaining 2 tablespoons of oil to the pot and fry for 5 minutes, stirring occasionally, taking care not to burn the peas. Add ⅓ cup of water if needed.

To serve, ladle the peas into bowls and serve hot with a heaping portion of greens of your choice.

Ingredient Highlight: Cumin and cumin seeds have a history of being used as a nutraceutical ingredient in Middle Eastern cuisine as well as being used as an antiseptic and disinfectant throughout India. Cumin has been seen to exert an antimicrobial effect on certain bacteria responsible for food spoilage.

Historical Highlights of

THE AMERICAN SOUTH

The story of the American South over the past several hundred years can be told through food. It's a history stained by the cruelty and harshness of racism, sexism, and classism; but throughout it all, a strong connection to place, to family, and to the flavors of home persists in its food.

Centuries ago, enslaved African people brought the flavors of home across the Atlantic. They cultivated and cooked with beans, melons, seeds, and rice—these were among the quintessential foods that made the transatlantic trip. Stateside, food combinations were born out of preservation and necessity. Crops like collards were similar to plants grown in Africa and became important to local foodways. Pigs became the livestock of choice as they were easy and relatively inexpensive to raise, and their pork could be salted and smoked, a form of preservation that increased shelf life. Indeed, many of these dishes (in traditional forms or reimagined) still regularly appear on restaurant and home-kitchen tables today.

In areas around Louisiana, Creole cuisine emerged as people with West African, French, Spanish, Caribbean, and Indigenous American roots fused their culinary techniques. Food culture in the South is varied and shifts as you move through regions. There is, however, a complexity, and food culture remains divided along race and class lines, an inheritance from the structures and systems of a bygone era. Still, in cities from Atlanta to New Orleans, restaurants and home cooks continue to innovate while holding true to their family traditions. The backbone of American food, Southern cuisine is ever evolving.

SALAD NIÇOISE *(France)*

This well-known salad is named for its city of origin, Nice, along the Côte d'Azur. The coastal region is home to some of the most beautiful Mediterranean vistas. Enjoying this salad, especially on a sunny day, may transport you on a mini vacation. Crunchy greens, jammy eggs, and a touch of the ocean make it nourishing and pure deliciousness.

24 fingerling potatoes (about 1 pound)

6 large eggs

1 pound fresh green beans, cleaned

Sprinkle of kosher salt

16 ounces fresh tuna, cleaned

3 large heirloom tomatoes, cut into 6 wedges each

1 head radicchio, castelfranco, or treviso

2 heads little gem lettuce, cleaned

1 cup kalamata olives, crushed

2 sprigs fresh basil

For the dressing

4 wild anchovies

Juice and zest of 2 lemons

⅔ cup extra-virgin olive oil

¼ cup chopped fresh basil

Sprinkle of kosher salt

⅛ teaspoon freshly ground black pepper

In a large stockpot, bring 4 quarts of water to a boil over high heat. Add the potatoes and boil for 10 minutes. Remove the potatoes and slice lengthwise, leaving the water in the pot.

Add the eggs to the same pot and cook for 6 minutes. Carefully remove the eggs and set aside. Once cool, peel the eggs and slice into halves.

Add the green beans to the same pot of water and cook uncovered for 4 minutes. Meanwhile, set up an ice bath in a large bowl. Remove the green beans from the water and place in the ice bath for 10 minutes, until they cool down. (This helps the green beans retain their vibrant green color.)

Lightly salt the tuna.

In a 6-inch cast-iron skillet over high heat, add the tuna and cook for 1 minute on each side. Remove and let cool for 2 minutes, then slice into 1-inch-thick strips.

Meanwhile, make the dressing: Combine in a small food processor the anchovies, lemon juice and zest, olive oil, basil, salt, and pepper. Pulse until all the ingredients are well combined.

In a large mixing bowl, place the green beans, tomatoes, and potatoes. Generously dress the vegetables, then gently toss until all the ingredients are well coated.

To serve, plate the radicchio, little gem lettuce, olives, and basil and add the green bean mixture, eggs, and tuna.

Ingredient Highlight: Anchovies are a rich source of protein and heart-healthy omega-3 fatty acids as well as a good source of iron and vitamins A and D, all important for cardiovascular as well as whole-body health.

GEMISCHTER SALAT *(Switzerland)*

(MIXED SALADS)

Taking a lunch break is a significant part of Swiss culture. This always gave me great pleasure to see people meeting midday at restaurants, where there is a choice of menus offering warm and cold meals. Among my favorites is the mixed salad plate that is made with an assortment of vegetable-based salads all plated together for a colorful and texture-filled meal. All of the salads can be enjoyed alone or together.

For the corn salad

4 cups corn kernels, cut from about 4 fresh large ears of corn

1 small shallot, finely sliced

Splash of apple cider vinegar

Crème fraîche

For the beet salad

4 beets, thinly sliced

1 tablespoon balsamic vinegar

¼ cup fresh dill

For the carrot salad

10 ounces shredded carrots

2 tablespoons white balsamic vinegar

⅓ cup extra-virgin olive oil

Pinch of kosher salt

Freshly ground black pepper to taste

For the cucumber salad

1 English cucumber, thinly sliced with skin on

1 Vidalia onion, thinly sliced

½ teaspoon kosher salt

For the baby greens salad

1 teaspoon Dijon mustard

¼ cup extra-virgin olive oil

⅛ cup apple cider vinegar

10 ounces mixed baby greens

⅓ cup fresh chives, coarsely chopped

1 bunch fresh parsley, coarsely chopped

Make the corn salad: In a medium bowl, place the corn and set aside. Combine the shallots and vinegar in a small bowl, allowing it to sit for 5 minutes. Add the shallots and vinegar to the corn and fold the crème fraîche into the corn.

Make the beet, carrot, and cucumber salads: Combine all the ingredients for each salad into a small bowl, mix well, and set aside.

Make the baby greens salad: Combine the mustard, olive oil, and vinegar in a mason jar and shake vigorously. Dress the greens, chives, and parsley and toss gently.

To serve, place a heaping spoon of each salad on a large plate and enjoy.

Ingredient Highlight: Betalain, a water-soluble pigment, is responsible for the signature red color that is unique to beets. Beets are a great source of fiber, potassium, and vitamin C, all of which are essential when managing blood sugars and blood pressure.

VEGETARIAN ZÜCHER GESCHNETZELTES

(Switzerland) **Serves 4**

(VEGETARIAN SLICED "MEAT")

Swiss cuisine is influenced by neighboring countries, and the flavors shift depending on where you are in the country. This dish originated in Zurich in the late 1940s, influenced by German and French cuisine, and is usually made with veal. I've substituted mushrooms to maintain the meaty texture. In addition to their delicious taste, mushrooms' meat-like texture makes them an excellent plant-based substitute. Enjoy this with rösti, a Swiss potato pancake.

⅓ bunch fresh sage

3.5 ounces oyster mushrooms

8 ounces baby bella mushrooms

8 ounces baby shiitake mushrooms

1 teaspoon kosher salt

¼ cup all-purpose flour

¼ cup all-purpose einkorn flour

⅔ cup avocado oil

2 tablespoons olive oil

1 large shallot, thinly sliced

2 garlic cloves, thinly sliced

¼ cup extra-dry vermouth

¼ cup heavy cream

Potatoes or rice, for serving

In a medium bowl, combine the sage, mushrooms, salt, and flours and toss until the sage and mushrooms are coated.

In a large sauté pan over medium heat, add the avocado oil. Gently pan-fry the sage and mushrooms about 5 minutes, or until crispy, and transfer them to a towel-lined sheet pan to drain the oil.

To the same sauté pan, add the olive oil, shallot, and garlic, then cook for 3 to 5 minutes, until translucent. Add the vermouth and cook for 2 minutes more.

Add the mushrooms and stir to combine. Then add the heavy cream and combine.

Spoon the mushrooms and fried sage onto a plate. Serve with potatoes or rice.

Ingredient Highlight: Sunny mushrooms—mushrooms that have been exposed to sunlight or UV light—can be a plant-based source of vitamin D. Mushrooms contain ergosterol, and when exposed to light, they can produce vitamin D.

EGGAH *(Middle East + North Africa)*

(EGYPTIAN-STYLE OMELET)

Inspired by nourishing Egyptian breakfasts, this baked omelet brings together and celebrates a diversity of flavors and textures along with a hearty serving of veggies. This version adds Tabasco sauce as a nod to African American traditions of serving hot sauce with eggs.

---

7 large eggs

¼ cup cream

⅛ cup sour cream

5 dashes Tabasco

1 tablespoon ground cumin, toasted

1 teaspoon sumac

1 tablespoon sriracha

¼ teaspoon kosher salt, plus more as needed

1 teaspoon freshly ground black pepper, plus more as needed

½ cup diced squash

½ cup diced zucchini

1 tablespoon ghee

2 beefsteak tomatoes, seeded and diced

1 bunch fresh parsley, chiffonade

⅛ cup cooked and cooled bulgur wheat or quinoa

4 tablespoons mint, thinly sliced

Juice and zest of 1 lemon

2 teaspoons apple cider vinegar

3 tablespoons extra-virgin olive oil

Preheat the oven to 380°F.

In a large bowl, whisk heavily the eggs, cream, and sour cream. This may be done by hand or with an electric mixer. Season with Tabasco, cumin, sumac, sriracha, salt and pepper, then set aside.

In a nonstick ovenproof skillet over medium-high heat, sauté the squash and zucchini with the ghee for about 5 minutes, or until brown. Add the egg mixture and immediately place in the oven. Bake for 12 to 18 minutes, until the eggs are golden and fully set. Test the middle with a toothpick or fork at 10 minutes to gauge how much time is left.

While baking the omelet, in a large bowl, mix the tomatoes, parsley, bulgur wheat, mint, lemon juice and zest, apple cider vinegar, and olive oil to make the parsley salad. Season it with salt and pepper to taste.

To serve, flip the omelet out of the pan onto a plate. Cut the omelet into triangle wedges and place on a plate. Spoon the parsley salad next to the omelet and enjoy immediately.

Nutrition Tip: This recipe is packed with fiber! The vegetables in this recipe are rich with soluble fiber and can slow down the absorption of sugar and help improve blood-sugar levels.

Ingredient Highlight: Sumac is a flowering shrub native to tropical climates and the Mediterranean. In addition to being a great source of antioxidants, it has been shown to reduce muscle pain after exercise.

 MEZZE *(Middle East + North Africa)*

CUCUMBER ZA'ATAR, LEMONY LABNEH, AND SPICED OLIVES

Mezze, which are small plates or appetizers, can be combined in a variety of ways and enjoyed with a small or large group. The best mezze platters play with savory and sweet flavors as well as temperature and texture. The herby flavor of za'atar is nicely tempered by the slightly sweet labneh, a strained-yogurt cheese, and a salty bite of olive.

4 Persian cucumbers, thinly sliced on a bias

3 heirloom tomatoes, coarsely chopped (about 1½-inch pieces)

½ red onion, thinly sliced

3 tablespoons extra-virgin olive oil

¼ teaspoon flaky sea salt, such as Maldon

2 tablespoons za'atar

Juice and zest of 2 lemons

2 cups labneh, or 1½ cups whole-milk yogurt plus ½ cup plain sour cream

2 tablespoons honey

2 sprigs fresh mint, leaves torn

2 cups Mediterranean olives with pits

Lebanese Bread (page 59), for serving

Storage Tip: The cucumber salad can be made in advance and stored in an airtight container in the refrigerator for 3 to 5 days. Feeling fancy? Top with a poached egg for a savory breakfast.

Place the cucumbers, tomatoes, and onion in a medium bowl with 2 tablespoons of the olive oil, the salt, za'atar, and half the lemon juice. Combine and set aside.

In another medium bowl, combine the labneh with the remaining lemon juice and honey. Mix well, garnish with mint, and set aside.

In a small bowl, combine the olives and lemon zest.

To serve, place a heaping dollop of cucumber and tomato alongside a heaping dollop of labneh. Make a well in the labneh and fill with the remaining olive oil. Enjoy family-style alongside the olives and Lebanese Bread.

HUMMUS *(Middle East + North Africa)*

Makes 1 quart (4 cups)

WITH BLACK SESAME TAHINI

You may be thinking, who needs another hummus recipe? The answer is, you do, and especially this one with black sesame tahini. Black sesame seeds impart a nutty flavor and are sourced from unhulled black sesame seeds. The color of this tahini is a conversation starter and will add a pop to any plate.

½ cup black sesame seeds

4 garlic cloves

1 cup extra-virgin olive oil

3 cups cooked chickpeas

Juice of 4 lemons

¼ teaspoon freshly ground black pepper

¼ teaspoon kosher salt

Mezze platter or flatbread, for serving (optional)

Preheat the oven to 325°F. Place the sesame seeds on a sheet pan and toast for 5 minutes.

Place the garlic, toasted sesame seeds, and olive oil in a blender and blend for 90 seconds. Add the chickpeas, lemon juice, black pepper, and salt and blend for another 2 to 3 minutes, until very smooth.

To serve, add a spoonful of hummus to your mezze platter or enjoy alone with flatbread.

Ingredient Highlight: Black sesame seeds are a good source of minerals, both macro and trace ones. Nondairy consumers rejoice as they provide a good dose of calcium! And just 2 tablespoons contain 83 percent of the daily recommended value of copper. Copper is a trace mineral that is needed to make energy and maintain the nervous and immune systems, and it is crucial in brain development.

FALAFEL *(Middle East + North Africa)*

It is said that falafel originated in Egypt in modern times, and it continues to be regularly enjoyed throughout Northern Africa, the Middle East, and around the globe. In fact, when I was training for the Boston Marathon (I ran for charity, so no, I'm not a superfast runner), falafel was my go-to recovery food—as a vegetarian at the time, I was always looking for good sources of plant-based proteins. This version relies on both fava beans and chickpeas and gets its bright green color from a heaping portion of parsley.

2 cups peeled, dried fava beans, prepared according to the package directions

2 cups drained, canned, or boxed chickpeas

1 cup chickpea flour

3 teaspoons baking soda

4 small garlic cloves

1 medium yellow onion

2 teaspoons dried coriander

1 teaspoon red chili powder

1 teaspoon freshly ground black pepper

1 teaspoon cumin powder

Kosher salt to taste

2½ cups fresh cilantro

1 large bunch fresh parsley

Extra-virgin olive oil

Mezze and flatbread of your choice, for serving

In a food processor fitted with a large blade attachment, place the fava beans and process them for 60 to 90 seconds until a paste is formed. Add the chickpeas and process for about 3 minutes, or until smooth. Add the chickpea flour, baking soda, garlic, onion, coriander, chili powder, black pepper, cumin, and salt, then process for another 3 minutes, until smooth and well combined into a coarse paste. Add the cilantro and parsley and process another 3 minutes, until well combined; the paste will be light green.

Transfer the paste to a sheet pan and spread out. Refrigerate for at least 1 hour, allowing the paste to cool down and the flavors to come together.

Preheat the oven to 350°F. Remove the sheet pan from the refrigerator and line another sheet pan with olive oil. Use an ice cream scoop to scoop a ball and, with clean hands, roll it back and forth. Flatten the ball and set aside on the prepared sheet pan. Repeat with the remaining paste until no more remains—you should have enough to make 20 to 23 falafel.

Bake for 10 minutes, flip each falafel, and bake for an additional 10 minutes.

To serve, enjoy 3 or 4 falafel with mezze and flatbread of your choice.

Nutrition Tip: When using canned, jarred, or boxed chickpeas, rinse them prior to cooking if you want to reduce your salt intake. Salt is often used as a preservative and flavor enhancer in canned, jarred, and boxed beans, but rinsing the beans helps remove the excess salt, and for those who are salt sensitive, reduces spikes in blood pressure.

CAPONATA *(Italy)*
WITH DUCK EGGS

Caponata is a Sicilian dish centered around eggplant. With a spread-like consistency, caponata can be paired with almost anything, served atop a slice of crusty fresh bread, enjoyed as an appetizer, or paired as an accompaniment to a main meal. This version reimagines breakfast, lunch, or brunch by serving the caponata with a duck egg.

½ cup plus 2 tablespoons extra-virgin olive oil, plus more for garnish

1 medium eggplant (about 1 pound), cut into small cubes

1 red onion, finely chopped

1 celery stalk, finely chopped

1 cup chopped cherry tomatoes

2 garlic cloves, crushed

½ teaspoon kosher salt, plus more as needed

¼ teaspoon freshly ground black pepper, plus more for garnish

1 tablespoon chopped cured black olives

1 teaspoon drained capers in brine

1 teaspoon red wine vinegar, plus more as needed

⅓ cup chopped fresh basil

4 duck eggs

1 sprig fresh basil, leaves torn, for garnish

2 tablespoons pine nuts, for garnish

Preheat the oven to 300°F.

In a large sauté pan over medium-high heat, add ½ cup of oil. Add the eggplant and cook for about 5 minutes, stirring a few times, until lightly browned and starting to soften and release its liquid.

Add the onion, celery, cherry tomatoes, garlic, salt, and pepper, and cook, stirring often for 8 to 10 minutes, until all the vegetables are softened. Add the olives, capers, and vinegar, stir, and remove from the heat. Stir in the basil. Taste and add more salt or vinegar as needed.

In a large skillet over medium heat, add the remaining 2 tablespoons of olive oil and crack the eggs directly into the pan. Fry until the desired consistency is reached.

To serve, plate the caponata, top with a fried duck egg, and garnish with basil, extra-virgin olive oil, black pepper, and pine nuts.

Ingredient Highlight: Duck eggs are an excellent source of high-value protein and a wonderful source of nutrients. Think of them as supercharged chicken eggs.

PORTUGUESE-STYLE EGGS

(Portugal)

Serves 6

These eggs are not hot enough to be called inferno eggs, as found in Italy, but they do have a kick thanks to the serrano peppers. Unlike some Portuguese-style recipes, these eggs are quickly made on the stovetop rather than in the oven but still have a smoky-and-sweet distinctive taste. If you like a lot of kick, add one more serrano pepper to the dish.

¼ cup extra-virgin olive oil

3 small rainbow bell peppers, diced

1 medium red onion, thinly sliced

4 garlic cloves, crushed

2 serrano peppers, seeded and julienned

¼ teaspoon kosher salt

1 tablespoon smoked paprika

3 ripe heirloom tomatoes, cut into 2-inch wedges

2 tablespoons fresh oregano leaves, torn

6 large eggs

¼ cup fresh basil leaves, for garnish

In a large cast-iron skillet over medium heat, place the olive oil, bell peppers, onion, garlic, serrano peppers, and salt and cook for 15 minutes. Add the paprika, tomatoes, and oregano, mix until combined, and cook for an additional 5 minutes, stirring occasionally.

Crack the eggs directly into the skillet, making a ring around the edges. Cover and reduce the heat to low and cook for 5 minutes.

To serve, plate a generous portion of sauce with 1 egg and garnish with fresh basil leaves.

Nutrition Tip: Eggs are a great source of essential nutrients that are beneficial for whole-body health. Current research supports consuming eggs as part of a healthy pattern of eating, and the good news is they don't seem to raise cholesterol when consumed in moderation.

FLAME-BROILED TOMATO

(West Coast US)

Serves 6 to 8

WITH ZUCCHINI BLOSSOMS

There is something about a baked tomato that brings the sweetness out in the most appetizing way. Fresh and in-season tomatoes are naturally sweet, and this recipe gives them space to shine. Lightly dressed with herbs, flowers, and black salt, it comes together with minimal effort. This pretty tomato will earn a space in your heart and regular meal rotation.

6 ripe tomatoes on the vine, cut in half

¼ cup extra-virgin olive oil

⅛ teaspoon Hawaiian black salt

3 spring onions, finely sliced

½ bunch fresh chives, finely chopped

7 basil leaves, finely chopped

½ cup apple cider vinegar

2 zucchini blossoms, thinly sliced

Ingredient Highlight: Hawaiian black salt, also known as black sea salt, has a similar nutrient profile to sea salt and imparts a smoky flavor. It can be found online or at specialty grocers.

Prep Tip: Zucchini blossoms can be purchased in the early summer at farmers' markets and year-round at specialty stores.

Preheat the oven to 350°F.

Arrange the tomatoes rounded side down on a sheet pan, drizzle with the olive oil, and sprinkle with the black salt. Bake for 35 to 40 minutes, or until the tomatoes are juicy and tender.

Meanwhile, add the onions, chives, basil leaves, and apple cider vinegar to a blender and purée until smooth. Remove the tomatoes from the oven and drizzle with the onion mixture and then top with the zucchini blossoms.

Serve warm and enjoy.

PIKLIZ

GRANNY DORO'S
SEASONING
Page 171

PIKLIZ *(Haiti)*
(PICKLED VEGETABLES)

Bring on the heat. Pikliz are a Haitian pickled staple made from a combination of cabbage, carrots, and some type of onion. You can use it as a seasoning on any dish that needs a little extra kick. Sometimes bell peppers are used in addition to the hot peppers. The key is to allow sufficient time for the pickle to cure, enabling the acid and heat to come together for a serious bite.

2½ cups thinly sliced cabbage

½ cup thinly sliced carrot, then cut into 1-inch pieces

½ cup thinly sliced shallots

4 to 5 habanero or Scotch bonnet peppers, stems removed, chopped

½ teaspoon coarse sea salt

1 cup white vinegar

1 cup rice vinegar

Pack the cabbage, carrot, shallots, peppers, and salt into a 4-cup (1-quart) mason jar. Pour both vinegars into the jar, cover, and seal.

Pikliz does not need to be refrigerated. Allow it to cure for at least 3 days and enjoy for up to 1 month.

Prep Tip: Make pikliz in bulk so you have some for yourself and some to share. They are delicious on everything from eggs to fish to avocado.

SUGO *(Italy)*
(SAUCE)

So often we purchase store-bought pasta sauces and are missing out on the incredible flavor of a sauce simmered on our own stovetop. The combination of vegetables and herbs makes for a smooth flavor profile. This recipe is far from intimidating and will become your preferred way to enjoy a sauce. Pair it with the pasta of your choice for a simple yet delicious meal.

Package of pasta of your choice

1 small carrot, coarsely chopped

1 celery stalk, coarsely chopped

1 small red onion, coarsely chopped

1 bunch fresh young basil, leaves and stems separated

1 garlic clove

¼ teaspoon kosher salt

4 tablespoons extra-virgin olive oil

¼ teaspoon chili flakes

1 (19.4-ounce) can Italian crushed *pelati* tomatoes

Cook the pasta according to the package directions and drain, reserving 1½ cups of the pasta water.

In a food processor, place the carrot, celery, onion, basil stems, and garlic and process until superfine.

In a medium stockpot over low heat, place the vegetables, salt, and olive oil and cook for 15 minutes uncovered.

Add the chili flakes and tomatoes, then add a little bit of water to the tomato can, swirl to get the sauce out, and add to the pot. Cook, covered, for 30 minutes over medium heat, stirring occasionally. Remove the lid and cook for an additional 60 minutes, stirring occasionally.

Thinly slice the basil leaves and mix half into the pot, saving the remaining leaves for garnish. Add 1½ cups of the pasta water, mix, and enjoy.

Ingredient Highlight: Onions hail from the allium family and are a rich source of organosulfur compounds and antioxidants that reduce free radical damage in the body.

Nutrition Tip: Using the salted pasta water helps cut down on the amount of salt needed in the recipe.

QUINOA CHAUFA *(Peru)*

(QUINOA FRIED "RICE")

This dish usually calls for rice that is then fried with a variety of vegetables. I've subbed in quinoa that is local to Peru along with yucca. It's a plant-protein-forward dish that is rich in fiber, vitamins, and minerals. You can increase the quantity when cooking and have enough for the whole week.

For the quinoa

2 tablespoons avocado oil

1½ cups black and white quinoa, really well rinsed until the water comes out clear

3 cups low-sodium vegetable stock

For the chaufa

4 tablespoons sesame oil

1 garlic clove, grated

1 large piece fresh ginger, peeled and grated

1 red bell pepper, chopped

1 yucca, boiled, cleaned, cored, and diced

1 bunch asparagus, chopped

3 thinly chopped scallions (green and white parts separated)

5 tablespoons low-sodium soy sauce

2 tablespoons vegetarian oyster sauce

1 small seedless jalapeño, chopped

2 avocados, peeled, pitted, and sliced, for garnish

2 sprigs fresh cilantro, for garnish

3 limes, for garnish

Make the quinoa: In a small stockpot over medium heat, add the oil and rinsed quinoa, and stir until it's hot. Then add the vegetable stock. Once it starts boiling, decrease the heat to low and cover. Cook for 15 to 20 minutes, until dry.

Remove the lid, fluff the quinoa with a fork, and let it dry out for a couple additional minutes. Set aside.

Make the chaufa: In a wok or large sauté pan over high heat, add the sesame oil, garlic, ginger, bell pepper, yucca, asparagus, and the white parts of the scallion. Sear all the vegetables for 3 to 4 minutes, then add the cooked quinoa. Try to get a little sear on the quinoa as well by not moving it in the pan.

Add the soy sauce, oyster sauce, and jalapeño. Cook for about 3 minutes until everything is well combined and has a nice crunch.

To serve, spoon the chaufa onto a plate and top with sliced avocado, cilantro, and a wedge of lime.

Ingredient Highlight: Native to the Andes region of South America, quinoa is a great choice if you are following plant-forward patterns of eating, as well as if you are thinking about your blood-sugar levels. Quinoa is packed with fiber and is a complete plant protein (meaning it has the whole amino acid profile), both of which are important in helping to support level blood sugars.

Peruvian cuisine has transformed over thousands of years as native indigenous cultures, colonization, slavery, indentured servitude, trade, and modernization left their imprint. Hugged by the Andes mountains, its diverse topography includes mountainous regions, large coastlines, arid areas, and rain forests, all home to incredible biodiversity.

Ancient civilizations included the Chavin, Moche, and Nasca, peoples who thrived on foods including ancient grains such as quinoa, choclo, wild meats, and seafood, depending on where they came from. One of the more well-known and documented ancient cultures is the Incan Empire. Ancient cooking techniques included cooking meats in the ground by creating pits that were heated by rocks, a tradition that persists today. The Spanish conquest toppled Incan rule, but by the early 1800s, Peru gained its independence. In the mid to late 1800s, Europeans from Italy and Germany immigrated to Peru, and indentured Cantonese workers arrived as well. With the influx of new cultures came flavors and foods that were representative of the immigrants' countries of origin.

Chifa, a marriage of Chinese and Peruvian cuisine, is one such example. Noodles, stir-fries, and dishes like the Peruvian stir-fry lomo saltado were created. People from Japan later migrated to Peru as contract workers on plantations. This birthed a painful and complicated history impacted by World War II and, after the war, decades of conflict and dictatorships. Again, the foodscape transformed to incorporate and use Japanese ingredients and cooking styles with traditional Peruvian ingredients.

TALLARINES VERDES *(Peru)*

Serves up to 8 people

(GREEN NOODLES)

These Peruvian green noodles are a take on Italian pesto, but this version is made with basil, spinach, and queso fresco. This delectable dish was the result of Italian migration from Leguria; in Peru, pesto transformed into a new dish that reflected the local foodways.

---

3 cups fresh basil leaves

2 cups baby spinach

½ cup fresh mint

½ cup walnuts

¾ cup cold-pressed extra-virgin olive oil

2 small garlic cloves

½ cup queso fresco

Package of linguine, whole wheat or chickpea

In a food processor, place the basil, spinach, mint, walnuts, olive oil, and garlic and blend for about 2 minutes, or until finely chopped and well combined. Transfer the pesto mixture to a small bowl and add the queso fresco, mixing well.

Cook the linguine according to the package instructions, drain, and dress with pesto.

To serve, plate the pasta and enjoy!

> **Prep Tip:** The pesto can be made ahead of time and stored for up to 2 days in the refrigerator until ready to use.

CUCUMBER AND WATERMELON SALAD

(Northeast US)

WITH LOBSTER

For me, lobster is synonymous with the Northeast of the United States, specifically Maine. For years on my birthday, I've returned to the Northeast and eaten lobster. The delicate yet distinctively sweet taste of lobster meat is the heart of this crisp salad. Filled with vitamins and minerals as well as protein, lobster is surely an ocean creature to love. Don't fret, you can substitute langoustine if you are unable to find lobster. The end result will be equally as delicious.

4 lobster or langoustine tails

¼ cup plus 1 tablespoon extra-virgin olive oil

Freshly ground black pepper to taste

1 lemon, cut in half

For the salad

¾ cup extra-virgin olive oil

¼ cup apple cider vinegar

1 tablespoon Dijon mustard

½ cup chopped fresh dill

¾ teaspoon kosher salt

2 English cucumbers (about 1 pound), peeled and thinly sliced

1 red scallion, red and green parts thinly sliced

1 bunch radishes, stems removed and thinly sliced

3 cups 1-inch-cubed seeded watermelon

To make the lobster tails, heat a stovetop grill over medium-high heat. Slice the lobster tails down the center, brush with olive oil, and place in a large bowl. Season with black pepper and set aside.

Grill the lemon halves for 2 minutes, until char marks are visible. Remove the lemons from the grill and set aside.

Grill the lobster for 8 to 10 minutes and set aside.

Make the salad: In a large bowl, whisk the oil, vinegar, mustard, dill, and salt. Add the cucumber, red scallion, and radish slices, toss to coat, and set aside for at least 5 minutes or up to 15 minutes. Add the watermelon cubes, set aside.

To serve, plate the salad and top with the lobster and a grilled lemon half on the side. You can squeeze the lemon over the salad, taking care not to eat the seeds, or slice and enjoy.

Nutrition Tip: If you are being mindful about how sodium shows up on your plate, you can omit the salt from the recipe and increase the acid from the apple cider vinegar and lemon as a bright and flavor-filled swap.

SAVORY SALAD (Northeast US)

WITH POMEGRANATE VINAIGRETTE

Escarole and endive are cool-weather vegetables that grow well in the northern part of the United States. In this salad, the bitter greens are tempered with the warmer notes of coriander, the sweetness of molasses, and mild mozzarella. From a health perspective, bitter greens are nutrient dense and support gut health and digestion.

For the dressing

2 garlic cloves, minced

4 serrano chilies, seeded and minced

½ teaspoon ground coriander, toasted

2 teaspoons pomegranate molasses

2 teaspoons fish sauce

2 tablespoons lime juice

1 tablespoon red wine vinegar

¼ cup extra-virgin olive oil

1 head escarole

1 head endive

Kosher salt

4 ounces mozzarella cheese, cut into small cubes

½ cup roasted cashews, coarsely chopped

Make the dressing: Combine the garlic, chilies, coriander, molasses, fish sauce, lime juice, and red wine vinegar as well as 1 tablespoon of water. Whisk in the oil.

Cut the greens into ribbons (a.k.a. chiffonade) and set them in a bowl. Add a pinch of salt, and pour some of the vinaigrette over the greens. Toss well and set aside.

Meanwhile, combine the cheese and cashews with the rest of the vinaigrette.

To serve, divide the dressed greens among 4 plates and top with the cheese and cashew mixture.

VEGETARIAN SHEPHERD'S PIE

(Central US)

The origins of shepherd's pie are said to date back to the 1700s, when cottage pie was created by Irish peasants out of a need to feed a family while minimizing food waste. This version is vegetable-forward. I invite you to empty your fridge of all the leftover veggies and add them to this dish.

Cooking spray

For the potatoes

1 pound russet potatoes, peeled and cut into 2-inch pieces

3 tablespoons unsalted butter

For the lentil sauce

2 tablespoons avocado oil

1 cup black sprouted lentils, prepared according to the package directions

1 small yellow onion, diced

3 garlic cloves, minced

2 tablespoons tomato paste

1 teaspoon dried oregano

2 teaspoons kosher salt

1 tablespoon balsamic glaze (can be found in the vinegar section)

½ cup red wine

2 medium carrots, diced

½ cup frozen baby peas

½ cup Cheddar cheese

For the béchamel

4 tablespoons (½ stick) unsalted butter

¼ cup all-purpose einkorn flour

1 cup buttermilk

½ teaspoon ground nutmeg

⅛ teaspoon kosher salt and freshly ground black pepper to taste

Preheat the oven to 350°F. Spray the bottom of a 2.5-quart casserole dish or a half-size foil pan with cooking spray.

Make the potatoes: In a large pot, add the potatoes and cover with cold water. Boil the potatoes until a paring knife inserted into the potatoes slides out easily. Strain the potatoes in a colander. Do not rinse. When the potatoes have cooled, mash them or use a potato ricer to break them up before returning them to the pot.

Add the butter and cook over medium heat for 3 minutes until combined and smooth (some small lumps are okay). Set aside.

Make the lentil sauce: Heat a large skillet over medium-high heat. Add the oil, lentils, onion, and garlic and cook for 5 to 6 minutes, until the onion is translucent.

Add the tomato paste, oregano, salt, balsamic glaze, wine, and carrots as well as 1½ cups of water to the pan. Reduce the heat to medium-low and cook for 20 minutes until the lentils are tender. Add more water if needed.

Add the baby peas and remove from the heat. Set aside.

Make the béchamel: In a small saucepan over medium heat, combine the butter and flour and cook for 4 minutes. Add the buttermilk and nutmeg and cook, stirring constantly for 3 to 4 minutes, until the béchamel is thick and creamy. Season with salt and pepper and set aside.

To assemble, set a casserole dish or half-size foil pan on a sheet tray lined with parchment paper. Spoon the lentil sauce on the bottom of the dish, then layer the potatoes on top. Pour the béchamel sauce on top of the potatoes and smooth out evenly. Finally, sprinkle the cheese on top.

Bake for 35 minutes until golden brown and bubbly. Allow to cool for at least 10 to 15 minutes before serving.

To serve, plate a generous portion of the pie and serve alongside the Savory Salad with Pomegranate Vinaigrette (page 146).

Prep Tip: To reduce the time spent on this recipe, use canned lentils instead of dry lentils. Rinse the lentils twice to reduce as much as 40 percent of the sodium in the can or, better yet, purchase low-sodium canned lentils!

RED LEAF LETTUCE AND FIG SALAD

(West Coast US)

Serves 6 to 8

WITH AVOCADO DRESSING

When you think of American West Coast cuisine, fresh *is often the first word that comes to mind, thanks to the abundance of fresh and local produce available. This salad is just that—a crisp and mouthwatering combination of fruits and vegetables. If you are unable to find pansies, you can substitute nasturtium, chamomile, lavender, or rose petals.*

---

4 heads red leaf lettuce, washed and torn into bite-size pieces

1 blood orange, peeled and seeded with the pith removed, sectioned, and cut in half

4 ounces black mission figs, cut into eighths

2 handfuls pansy flowers, for garnish

For the dressing

1 ripe avocado, halved and pitted

¼ cup extra-virgin olive oil

½ cup strawberry rosé vinegar or any botanical vinegar

Flaky sea salt, such as Maldon

In a large salad bowl, place the lettuce, oranges, and figs and gently toss.

Meanwhile, make the dressing: In a small food processor, add the avocado flesh, olive oil, and vinegar. Blend for 30 to 60 seconds. Sprinkle with flaky sea salt.

Dress the salad and gently toss. Arrange the pansies on top of the lettuce.

Ingredient Highlight: Edible flowers enhance the beauty of any dish and are also a good source of phenolic compounds that have antioxidant properties.

Prep Tip: You can find edible flowers during the summer months at your local farmers' market or year-round at specialty stores. Strawberry rosé vinegar can be purchased online.

GRILLED ARTICHOKE *(West Coast US)*

TOPPED WITH SPINACH WHIPPED GOAT CHEESE

Growing up, I was always fascinated with artichokes and loved dipping them in butter, especially the delicate center. At the time, I didn't know they were incredibly nutrient dense. This grilled version has a delicious bite especially when paired with spinach sauce as a dipping sauce or drizzled on top. You can make the lassi in advance and dress any grilled veggie of your choice.

6 artichokes, sliced lengthwise

¼ cup extra-virgin olive oil

For the spinach sauce

1 cup plain whole-milk yogurt

2 ounces goat cheese

⅛ teaspoon Himalayan or kosher salt

Freshly ground black pepper to taste

3 cups spinach, steamed

1 tablespoon honey

Place a steamer basket in a large pot and add enough water that it reaches below the basket. Bring the water to a boil and add the artichokes to the basket stem side up. Cover the pot and steam the artichokes for 25 to 30 minutes. You'll know the artichokes are finished when the hearts are tender and can be pierced easily with a fork.

Remove the artichokes from the pot, drain any excess water, and brush with the olive oil.

Heat a stovetop grill over medium-high heat. Place the artichokes flat-side down on the grill and grill for 7 to 10 minutes until char marks are visible. Remove and set aside.

Meanwhile, make the spinach sauce: In a blender, add the yogurt, goat cheese, salt, black pepper, spinach, honey, and 2 cups of water and purée.

To serve, pour the spinach sauce over the grilled artichokes and enjoy warm.

Ingredient Highlight: Artichoke is a good source of luteolin, an antioxidant that is involved in potentially lowering cholesterol and, in turn, reducing the risk of developing heart disease.

CALIFORNIA

California is home to both the highest and lowest land points in the lower forty-eight states, and its cuisine is just as wide-ranging. Spanish missionaries arrived via Mexico and displaced many of the Indigenous groups in present-day Southern California; their influence on food culture in the area is undeniable. The flavors of Baja California are prevalent throughout Southern California, with dishes like shrimp and fish tacos with shredded cabbage.

Russian groups settled in Northern California. Basque families from France and Spain moved to the eastern mountainous regions of the state, bringing their sheepherding skills and family-style meals featuring hearty stews with sweet peppers and Basque sheepherders bread. The gold rush in the mid-nineteenth century also brought people from all types of backgrounds seeking wealth and birthed dishes such as Hangtown fry. As the population and industry grew, Chinese laborers came to California to build the railroads. More recently, Vietnamese and Armenian communities have settled in LA.

As each group has arrived, it has brought the culinary ways from home and added to California's food culture. Known for its fresh health-forward global cuisine and pivotal role in food freedom and justice movements, California has become a leader of culinary innovation.

FISH

CHILI COCONUT CRAB RICE

(West and Central Africa)

Serves 6

Coconuts are reminiscent of coastal Africa and okra is a staple vegetable as well, both boasting an array of health-supporting nutrients. The use of vadouvan *curry imparts warm, sweet, and smoky notes all at once—while the crab brings the brine of the ocean. All of the components make for a nourishing and tummy-warming dish.*

1 cup rice grits

2 tablespoons vadouvan spice blend

Kosher salt

3 tablespoons unsalted butter

1 pound unpasteurized jumbo lump crabmeat

4 tablespoons dried Aleppo pepper

½ cup coconut oil

¾ cup avocado oil plus ¼ cup for frying

3 tablespoons benne seeds (also known as sesame seeds)

20 pieces thinly sliced okra

2 scallions, whites and greens, thinly sliced, for garnish

2 tablespoons minced chives, for garnish

⅛ teaspoon freshly ground black pepper

Ingredient Highlight: Botanically, okra is a fruit! It's an excellent source of vitamins C and K as well as being a good source of other vitamins, plant-based protein, and fiber. Current research has found that okra may help improve lipid profiles and blood sugars.

Make the rice: Rinse the rice until starch runs through. In a pot, place the rice and cover with water by at least 1 inch. Cook over high heat until the water boils, reduce to a simmer, cover with the lid, and cook for 14 to 15 minutes and check. Cook uncovered for an additional 3 minutes, until the water is fully absorbed.

Season with the vadouvan and salt to taste. Reserve, keeping it warm.

Make the crab: In a small pot, place the butter and ¼ cup of water and melt together, constantly whisking to emulsify.

Add the crab to the pot and warm through until hot.

Make the chili oil: In a blender, place 3 tablespoons of the Aleppo, the coconut oil, and ½ cup of the avocado oil. Blend for about 60 seconds, until fully incorporated. Add the remaining Aleppo and the benne seeds. Blend for an additional 30 seconds, then set aside.

Make the okra: Place the sliced okra in a heavy-bottomed medium skillet over high heat with avocado oil and fry for about 15 minutes, continuously stirring, or until crispy. Take care not to burn the okra. Set aside on a towel-lined pan to absorb the excess oil.

Recipe continues

FISH

To serve, place the rice on the bottom of each bowl. Gently spoon the crab across the top of the rice. Garnish with scallions and chives. Stir the chili oil and lightly dress the crab with oil. Place the okra sporadically across the top of the crab. Season with salt to taste and the pepper.

Low Country, a region along the South Carolinian coast and the Sea Islands of the United States, has a rich and painful history intertwined with the African continent. The crab in this dish is local to the Low Country waters—the key ingredients here are born out of the African diaspora, acknowledging the African lives that were used to build the US economy.

 # CEVICHE *(Peru)*

Peruvian ceviche, a dish of raw fish, is influenced by Japanese migration during the late eighteenth and nineteenth centuries, with the use of citrus coming from the Spanish colonization. The use of the herbs and choclo, a Peruvian corn, is a nod to the Indigenous peoples there. This recipe is usually made with aji amarillo, *a Peruvian yellow chili pepper. Here I've used habanero pepper in concert with nutrient-rich sweet potato and cilantro.*

---

1 red onion, thinly sliced

6 red snapper fillets, sushi-grade quality, cut into 1-inch cubes

Juice of 6 limes

Zest of 3 limes

1 habanero pepper, seeded and thinly sliced

3 sweet potatoes

1 bunch fresh cilantro, leaves and stems separated

1 tablespoon fish sauce

2 tablespoons extra-virgin olive oil

Package of choclo, prepared according to package directions

Lime wedges, for garnish

2 avocados, peeled, pitted, and cut into thirds, for garnish

In a small bowl, soak the red onion covered with cold water and ice for 30 minutes. Then drain and set aside in the refrigerator until ready to use.

In a medium bowl, combine the red snapper, lime juice, zest, and habanero, then set aside in the refrigerator for 15 minutes.

Meanwhile, boil the sweet potatoes in a medium stockpot for about 15 minutes, or until fork tender. Drain and slice in half lengthwise, then set aside.

Remove the fish from the refrigerator and drain the juice that has accumulated into a blender. Add the cilantro stems, ½ cup of the marinated fish, fish sauce, and olive oil and blend until smooth and well combined.

Add the blended fish to the red snapper and lime juice mixture, add the onion, and gently combine.

To serve, top half a sweet potato with a spoonful of ceviche and choclo on the side, then garnish with the cilantro leaves, lime wedge, and avocado.

Ingredient Highlight: Choclo, a large kernel Peruvian field corn, is a good source of fiber and is supportive of digestive health.

FISH

A Caribbean island with a rich and celebrated cultural history, Jamaica is home to rain forests, white beaches with coral reefs, mountains, and urban areas. Like its island cousins, Jamaica is no stranger to colonization and its impact on the Indigenous population.

The Arawak peoples experienced near destruction under Columbus, and the Taino people were enslaved by colonizers—both their imprints can be felt on Jamaica's foodscape today. Later, the Spanish government brought enslaved African people to the country. Each of these groups contributed different culinary practices to the island. Traditional Tainos cooking utilized all parts of the bitter cassava plant and introduced allspice to their colonizers. The Jamaican patty—a combination of meat, seafood, or vegetables heavily seasoned with garlic, thyme, allspice, or Scotch bonnet pepper—was born out of a mix of cultures and experiences. Techniques taken from African peoples melded with spices from indentured Indian laborers and then were adapted by the English.

The island's tumultuous and oppressive history made way for the Rastafarian movement in the 1930s, followed by reggae music in the 1960s, known as the voice of the oppressed. When you visit the island today, you will experience a plethora of flavors including jerk, a favorite of mine, a seasoning used as a marinade that combines sweet and spice as well as fresh herbs.

ESCOVITCH *(Jamaica)*

Serves 4

This dish is traditionally made with fried red snapper and generously topped with pickled escovitch sauce, similar to escabeche in Spain, South America, and the Philippines. I've substituted catfish fillets prepared in an air fryer in place of traditional frying methods and added ginger beer, a Jamaican favorite, for a sweet yet spicy kick.

For the fish

4 catfish fillets, cleaned

1 cup Granny Doro's Seasoning (page 171)

1 tablespoon avocado oil

Pinch of flaky sea salt, such as Maldon

Freshly ground black pepper to taste

For the escovitch

1 cup white vinegar

½ (4-ounce) can Jamaican ginger beer

2 tablespoons whole black peppercorns

1 teaspoon ground allspice

2 sprigs fresh thyme

1 small onion, thinly sliced

2 garlic cloves, thinly sliced

1 red bell pepper, thinly sliced

1 medium carrot, julienned

Prepare the fish: Score the fish on each side and season with Granny Doro's Seasoning. Marinate for at least 15 minutes.

Gently brush the exterior of the fish with the avocado oil and place the fish in the air fryer. Cook on 380°F for 4 to 5 minutes.

Make the escovitch: In a medium stockpot, place the vinegar, ginger beer, and black pepper. Bring to a boil and cook for 3 to 5 minutes. Add the allspice, thyme, onion, and garlic and cook for 5 minutes. Add the bell pepper and carrot and cook for 3 to 5 minutes, until the carrot is al dente.

To serve, plate the fish and generously dress with the escovitch. Finish with a sprinkle of flaky sea salt and freshly ground black pepper.

Substitution Tip: If you'd prefer to use red snapper, opt for red snapper that has been responsibly caught or sustainably managed.

Ingredient Highlight: Allspice, an aromatic spice, has been used for centuries throughout the Caribbean and in South America both in cooking as well as in medicine. The polyphenol eugenol, found in allspice, helps to stimulate digestive enzymes, aiding the digestive process and easing stomach pain.

FISH

GRILLED BASS (Brazil)
WITH GARLIC-HERB SAUCE

Seafood may not be top of mind when you think of Brazil. However, Brazilians do enjoy seafood thanks to its long coastal plain hugged by the Atlantic Ocean. This dish provides heart-healthy unsaturated fats found in fish along with phytonutrients and antioxidants. The flavors in this recipe come from the generous use of herbs and spices.

3 pounds basa or sea bass

1 cup plus 1 tablespoon extra-virgin olive oil

Kosher salt

1 cup firmly packed fresh flat-leaf parsley leaves

½ cup firmly packed fresh cilantro leaves

6 garlic cloves, minced

1 teaspoon freshly ground black pepper

¼ teaspoon red pepper flakes

Juice of 3 lemons

Ingredient Highlight: Thanks to its allicin content, garlic is a vasodilator that has the potential to lower blood pressure in individuals with high blood pressure.

Rinse and pat the fish dry then place on a sheet pan. Brush both sides with 1 tablespoon olive oil, season with a pinch of salt, and set aside.

Make the sauce: Finely chop the parsley, cilantro, and garlic (while this step *can* be done in a food processor, I recommend chopping by hand to ensure the herbs don't become mushy). Transfer to a small bowl and combine with 1 cup olive oil and the black pepper, red pepper flakes, and lemon juice as well as a pinch of salt. If not using the mixture immediately, cover and refrigerate. Allow the mixture to come to room temperature before serving.

Grill the fish: Heat an indoor or outdoor grill over medium-high heat. Grill the fish for 4 to 6 minutes per side, until done to your liking. Transfer the fish to a carving board and let it rest for 3 to 5 minutes before slicing. Cut diagonally across the grain into ¼-inch-thick slices.

To serve, arrange the sliced fish on a serving platter and drizzle with the sauce.

As the largest country in South America and the fourth largest country in the world, Brazil and its cuisine are as varied as its people. When the Portuguese arrived in Brazil in the 1500s, they brought with them enslaved Africans and settled in the northeastern region of Bahia. These European colonizers introduced salted cod, sweets, some fruits, and sugar that they collected on their conquests. During this time of European colonization, cattle were banished from Brazil, as they destroyed the sugarcane that served as the cash crop of the region. Foods such as palm oil, coconut, plantains, and okra were introduced by Africans, and their influences helped to create the much loved dish *feijoada*.

The humid tropical climate allows for an abundance of agricultural practices. Brazil is the world's leading producer of coffee, and about a third of the world's oranges are grown there. It's the world's main producer of cassava, which has been a vital part of the country's indigenous cuisine prior to Portuguese colonization. Cookware has also withstood the test of time, with the traditional earthenware water jug and wicker sieve of the Indigenous population still in use.

Influences from the Indigenous peoples, Africans, and Portuguese have shaped the Brazilian food system and influenced the sociopolitical systems. Regional differences also exist in Brazilian cuisine. The Amazon region continues to be representative of the region's first inhabitants. Cassava-based items such as *beijus*, a cracker sometimes flavored with coconut, are popular, as well as duck, fish from the river, and tropical fruits. With their large settlements of Italian and German immigrants, the southern states are more heavily swayed by European influences. The meat culture there is also much more abundant (think spit-roasting meat churrasco-style) as cattle farming is a major industry in that region.

GRANNY DORO'S SEASONING

(Trinidad and Tobago)

Makes about 1 cup

My granny always had a bottle of this homemade seasoning in her fridge, and it was the seasoning I requested most. She packed her seasoning with fresh herbs from her garden and made it without added salt. It's a delicious marinade for any protein or as an addition to a pot of veggies.

1 bunch celery, coarsely chopped

1 bunch fresh cilantro, coarsely chopped

2 garlic cloves, coarsely chopped

1 small yellow onion, coarsely chopped

1 pimento pepper, coarsely chopped

1 bunch fresh chives, coarsely chopped

1 bunch fresh basil, coarsely chopped

2 sprigs fresh thyme, leaves pulled off

1½ cups white vinegar

Freshly ground black pepper

In a blender, combine half of each of the celery, cilantro, garlic, onion, pimento, chives, basil, and thyme, and add the vinegar and ½ cup of water. Blend until minced but not puréed. Strain the mixture into a bowl, pressing on the solids to extract most of the liquid. Reserve the liquid and place the vegetables into another bowl.

Return the liquid to the blender, add the remaining ingredients, and blend to the same consistency as the first batch. Strain again, reserving the liquid. Add the second batch of vegetables to the first along with the liquid and a healthy dose of fresh black pepper and stir to combine.

Place the seasoning in a glass jar and store in the refrigerator, where it will keep for up to 2 months.

Tips: Use a wooden, ceramic, or plastic spoon to scoop out the seasoning, as metal can cause the seasoning to oxidize and turn. The vinegar preserves the seasoning, keeping it fresh for a couple of months in the refrigerator.

Nutrition Tip: Making your own seasoning is a great way to play with ingredients and flavors while reducing unwanted additives. Store-bought seasonings and condiments tend to be high in sodium and can be an unexpected source of added sugars. Keep a jar of this seasoning in your refrigerator to use with different recipes.

FISH

SALTED COD *(Trinidad and Tobago)*

Salted cod is a popular breakfast dish in Trinidad and Tobago that is often made with vegetables, fresh herbs, and spices. It may be served with bake—a quick bread—or boiled dumplings and a dollop of pepper sauce. I like to pair mine with bake as well as avocado and cucumber. Full of flavor and easy to prepare, this savory breakfast is perfect for a large crowd.

2 pounds salted cod (see Note)

2 tablespoons avocado oil

1 red onion, thinly sliced

2 garlic cloves, minced

3 tomatoes, diced

3 ribs celery, diced

1 green bell pepper, diced

1 red bell pepper, diced

1 yellow bell pepper, diced

3 sprigs thyme

Freshly ground black pepper

Ingredient Highlight: Thyme, a fragrant herb, holds its own when it comes to its nutrient profile. When consumed in large quantities, it's an antioxidant-rich source of vitamin C and a good source of fat-soluble vitamin A, both of which support immune function.

In a large bowl, place the salted cod, cover with room temperature water, and soak for a minimum of 2 hours or overnight, covered on the countertop.

Drain and reserve 1 cup of the water to be used during the cooking process.

Heat a 9-inch cast-iron skillet over medium heat and add the oil, onion, and garlic. Cook for 3 to 5 minutes, taking care not to burn the garlic.

Add the tomatoes and cook for 3 minutes. Stir the celery and peppers into the mixture and cook for 3 minutes. Next, gently rub the thyme between your hands over the pan and allow the leaves to fall in. If the mixture is dry, add 2 tablespoons of the reserved water for moisture. Cook for an additional 5 to 7 minutes.

Add the cod, stirring until combined, and cook for an additional 3 to 5 minutes. Season with black pepper to taste.

To serve, place a few spoonfuls of the cod on a plate with a drizzle of your favorite hot sauce alongside a green salad with a slice of Coconut Bake (page 57).

Note: If you are short on time, in a large stockpot, place the salted cod over high heat and boil for 10 minutes. Drain and add fresh water, bringing to a boil for an additional 10 minutes. Drain again and add fresh water, bringing to a boil for an additional 15 minutes. Drain and reserve 1 cup of the water to be used during the cooking process.

GRAVLAX *(Scandinavia)*

(CURED SALMON)

The first time I made gravlax, a type of cured salmon, was with one of my closest friends, Marsa, who is quite the home cook. She talked about growing up in a Finnish-Austrian home where dishes like gravlax and mustard were always made from scratch. Cooking at home was a staple in her family. This dish is surprisingly simple and quite flavorful. If you prefer a hard cure, you can leave the fish to set for 24 to 30 hours.

2½ cups coconut sugar

3¾ cups kosher salt

⅓ cup dried fennel

¼ cup whole black peppercorns

1 (4- to 5-pound) fillet of salmon

2 bunches fresh dill

2 bunches fresh tarragon

Fresh peels from 1 lemon

In a medium bowl, combine the sugar, salt, fennel, and peppercorns. Sprinkle about a third of the mixture at the bottom of a parchment-lined baking pan.

Place the salmon fillet skin-side down on top of the mixture. Top it with the dill, tarragon, and lemon peels.

Wrap the salmon tightly with parchment paper, cover the dish, and refrigerate for 24 hours. Check the salmon at the halfway mark and drain and discard any liquid that may have accumulated.

To serve, thinly slice the gravlax on an angle with a very sharp knife, taking care not to cut the skin. Cover any part of the remaining gravlax with the excess skin and store in the refrigerator for up to 7 days.

Ingredient Highlight: Salmon is an excellent source of the omega-3 fatty acids EPA and DHA, which support blood vessel health and reduce systemic inflammation. It is also an excellent source of B vitamins, which are important for the central nervous system.

Ingredient Highlight: Tarragon in large quantities on a regular basis helps the body to sensitize insulin, especially for people who are experiencing impaired glucose tolerance. It also helps to increase HDL-C, the cardio-protective form of cholesterol.

Weather and location play important roles in the food culture of Scandinavia, with its landscape shaped by the rugged terrain across the north and milder climate in the coastal areas. Along the coasts of Norway, Denmark, Finland, and Sweden, fish is featured prominently on plates every day, while meat and game are more common inland.

With extreme cold across the north and relatively short fishing seasons, Scandinavian cuisine has long featured preserved foods such as dried reindeer, salt cod and salt pork, and smoked fish. The raids and exploration during the Viking and Middle Ages helped expand the availability of other foods. Archaeological excavations have found that Viking meals consisted of fermented dairy products; wild fruits including berries; vegetables like beans, onions, and cabbage; nuts; rye and sourdough bread; boiled meats (pork, horse, sheep, and goat); as well as freshwater and ocean fish. Food was abundant and often paired with fermented alcohol. More affluent people in this time were thought to have access to preserved meats, as salt was a luxury.

Flavor combinations such as allspice and preserved berries can be found in dishes like *kroppkakor*, a potato dumpling filled with meat, seasoned with allspice, and garnished with lingonberries. Meatballs (page 200) also feature a combination of allspice and berries. Crayfish parties have been enjoyed in Sweden since the 1500s; they are much like the crawfish boils enjoyed in the American South.

POISSON GROS SEL *(Haiti)*

(RED SNAPPER WITH COARSE SALT)

Serves 2 to 4

Fried snapper is a childhood favorite of mine. I would always ask my stepmother, Florienne, to make it for me. Now don't be frightened by the whole fish! This recipe makes preparing a whole fish approachable so you will return to it time and time again.

---

2 pounds whole red snapper, cleaned (depending on the size, may be 1 large fish or 2 small fish)

1 lime, cut in half

1 medium sweet yellow onion, coarsely chopped

Juice of 2 limes

2 scallions, chopped

3 garlic cloves

2 tablespoons fresh flat-leaf parsley

1 teaspoon fresh thyme

2 teaspoons flaky sea salt, such as Smoked Maldon

½ cup all-purpose flour

½ cup avocado oil

1 habanero or Scotch bonnet pepper, quartered

3 tablespoons unsalted butter

1 cup white wine

½ cup sliced shallots

½ cup julienned red or orange bell pepper

½ bunch fresh parsley, coarsely chopped

Rinse the fish with cold water. Remove any remaining scales and rinse the cavity. Rub the lime halves all over the fish with a gentle scrubbing motion.

Score the fish with several 2- to 3-inch slits on both sides. Lay the fish flat in an airtight container and place in the refrigerator.

Meanwhile, in a blender or food processor, add the onion, lime juice, scallions, garlic, parsley, thyme, and salt. Blend or pulse on low speed just until combined. The marinade will be thick.

Pour the marinade over the fish, making sure it is fully coated. Reseal the container and allow the fish to marinate in the refrigerator for at least 3 hours (up to overnight).

To prepare the fish, remove the fish from the marinade and shake off the excess. Keep the remaining marinade to the side. Dredge the fish in the flour.

To cook the fish, in a nonstick skillet over medium-high heat, add the oil. Once the oil shimmers, gently place the fish in the pan. Cook in the oil for 3 to 5 minutes on each side, until golden brown and lightly crispy. Remove the fish from the pan. Drain on a plate lined with a paper towel.

Remove any excess oil from the pan. Return the pan to the stove and add the reserved marinade, along with the habanero pepper, butter, and wine. Cook over medium heat for 5 to 7 minutes. Add the shallots and bell pepper and cook for 2 minutes more.

To serve, spoon the sauce over the prepared fish and garnish with the chopped parsley.

Nutrition Tip: Red snapper is a great source of heart-healthy fats, specifically omega-3 fatty acids, which support a reduction in the development of blood clots, high blood pressure, inflammation, and low-density lipoprotein, LDL, or "bad" cholesterol.

FISH

POLVO *(Portugal)*

(OCTOPUS) WITH POTATOES, CELERY, AND OLIVES

Either you love octopus, or polvo *in Portuguese, or you don't. This one is for the polvo lovers and polvo-curious home cooks. The dish takes some time and attention to prepare but it is well worth the effort as the end result will make you feel like you have left your kitchen and are dining at the chef's table. I encourage you to invite your friends over to enjoy the final result.*

---

10 stalks of celery (5 external parts only, coarsely chopped, and 5 center parts with leaves, cut on the bias)

1 medium yellow onion, cut in half with the skin

2 lemons, cut in half

9 fresh bay leaves

½ bunch fresh parsley, stems and leaves separated

1 tablespoon whole black peppercorns

2 corks

4 pounds octopus tentacles

1 pound fingerling potatoes

½ teaspoon kosher salt, plus more for finishing

Juice of 2 lemons

2 tablespoons smoked paprika

½ cup extra-virgin olive oil

1 cup crushed Galega or kalamata olives

Freshly ground black pepper, for finishing

Chili oil, for finishing

In a 9-quart stockpot over medium-high heat, place the external parts of the celery, the onion, lemon, 5 of the bay leaves, parsley stems, black peppercorns, and corks, cover with water, and bring to a boil.

Add the octopus tentacles, cover, reduce the heat to medium-low, and cook for 45 minutes, ensuring that the octopus is covered all the way through.

Meanwhile, in a medium stockpot, place the fingerling potatoes, the remaining 4 bay leaves, and salt, cover with water, and bring to a boil. When the potatoes are fork tender, drain and place into a large bowl.

When the octopus is ready, drain the octopus and then cut the tentacles in half and set aside.

Add the octopus to the large bowl with the potatoes, along with internal parts of the celery, lemon juice, paprika, olive oil, and olives. Massage the ingredients together and set aside.

To serve, season with salt, black pepper, and chili oil (see page 159), and serve warm topped with parsley leaves.

Sourcing Tip: If you are unable to find fresh octopus, swap in frozen that has been defrosted in the refrigerator. Opt for responsibly caught octopus.

SHRIMP *(the Philippines)*
ARROZ CALDO
(SHRIMP RICE STEW)

In the Philippines, this dish is like their version of chicken noodle soup. However, it does not contain chicken or noodles but holds a similar sentimental value. Instead the soup combines rice and a lot of ginger as well as shrimp for an incredibly nourishing soup that can be enjoyed any time of day. The soup can be garnished with fresh herbs, soft-boiled eggs, toasted garlic, or anything your taste buds desire.

½ cup glutinous rice

1 tablespoon avocado oil

4 tablespoons minced fresh garlic

8 tablespoons minced sweet onion

8 tablespoons minced fresh ginger

½ cup jasmine rice

1 tablespoon fish sauce, plus more for serving

Pinch of white pepper

Pinch of kosher salt

8 cups low-sodium shrimp stock

1 ounce saffron, plus more as desired (optional)

1 large egg, at room temperature

Ingredient Highlight: Glutinous rice, contrary to how it sounds, is gluten-free! It has a lower amylose content in comparison to other rice and does not require as much liquid to cook. The end consistency is a wonderfully sticky rice.

1 pound shrimp, peeled, deveined, and cut into chunks (keep heads and shells if making stock)

1 soft-boiled egg, for serving

Scallions, coarsely chopped, for serving

Toasted garlic, for serving

Garlic oil, for serving (optional)

Calamansi or lemon, for serving (optional)

Crumbled chicharron, for serving (optional)

In a medium bowl, place the glutinous rice and cover with water overnight. Drain and discard the water and set the rice aside.

Preheat the oven to 350°F.

In a large ovenproof pot, add the oil and sauté the garlic, onions, and ginger on medium heat for 3 to 5 minutes, stirring often, until the vegetables become translucent.

Add the glutinous and jasmine rice and cook for 3 to 4 minutes, stirring occasionally. Add the fish sauce, white pepper, and salt and stir to combine.

Next add the shrimp stock and the saffron (if using) and stir until the stock is simmering. Cover the pot and place in the oven for 45 minutes.

Remove the pot from the oven and place on the stove over low heat.

FISH

Recipe continues

In a small bowl, beat the egg. Scoop 1 cup of arroz caldo into the bowl and stir very quickly to temper the egg and prevent curdling. The mixture should be warm, but if not, add more arroz caldo.

Pour the egg mixture and the raw shrimp into the pot and stir for 2 to 6 minutes, or until the shrimp are pink.

To serve, spoon the arroz caldo into a bowl and top with a soft-boiled egg, the scallions, the toasted garlic, and any of the other garnishes, as desired. Enjoy warm.

Filipino cuisine is shaped by influences as numerous as the 7,000 islands that comprise the nation. Its location put it in the path of migration and trade for thousands of years—Chinese traders, Spanish conquistadors led by Portuguese navigator Ferdinand Magellan, and Spanish colonizers who settled in the islands for more than 300 years.

Filipino cuisine often combines four distinct flavors: salty, sweet, sour, and bitter. You can find this unmistakable taste in the combination of sour green mango with fermented fish paste. Bitter melon, taro, swamp cabbage, and mung beans are regularly used in the cuisine, as is rice, brought to the region by ancient trading routes.

Trade not only introduced new ingredients but also ways of cooking, such as a method of preserving meat in vinegar and spices known as adobo (Filipino Pork Adobo, page 198). Historically, caste systems dictated the traditional eating patterns, as members of the upper class dined on meat and dairy products introduced by the Spanish while working-class Filipinos consumed food influenced by Chinese traders, especially rice-based dishes. The Filipino food that exists today is a blend of traditional Asian and European cuisine.

SEA SCALLOPS AND ASPARAGUS

(Northeast US)

More often than not, scallops are an environmentally sustainable seafood choice that are incredibly quick to prepare and have the most buttery yet slightly briny flavor. An excellent source of omega-3 fatty acids and protein, scallops make any dish sing, so they are perfect for special occasions or gatherings with those you love.

Kosher salt

2 pounds sea scallops

1 tablespoon avocado oil

For the asparagus

1 tablespoon extra-virgin olive oil

1 Vidalia onion, thinly sliced

Pinch of flaky sea salt, such as Maldon

3 sprigs fresh tarragon

8 ounces snap peas

1 cup low-sodium vegetable broth

3 bunches asparagus, trimmed and cut on a bias

Salt the sea scallops.

Heat a heavy-bottomed pot over high heat until very hot. Add the oil and scallops, taking care not to overcrowd the pan. Sear for 2 minutes and then turn over, cooking for an additional 30 to 60 seconds.

Make the asparagus: In a heavy-bottomed pan over medium heat, add the olive oil and onion and cook for 5 to 7 minutes, until slightly golden but not burned. Add a pinch of flaky salt.

Add the tarragon and snap peas and cook for 5 to 7 minutes. Then, add ¼ cup of the broth and cook for 5 minutes.

Add the asparagus and the remaining ¾ cup of broth, and cook for 5 minutes uncovered.

To serve, place 4 scallops on a plate with asparagus, then gently drizzle the asparagus with the broth, onions, and snap peas.

Nutrition Tip: Most of the sodium we consume doesn't come from the salt shaker but from packaged goods. If you don't make your own broths, opt for a low- or reduced-sodium option to support your cardiometabolic health.

FISH

MEAT

PELAU *(Trinidad and Tobago)*
(PILAF)

This one-pot dish is a crowd-pleaser that can be made in advance and gets better as the days go on. Everyone has their own special technique when it comes to making pelau; when I walked a plate of mine over to my neighbor who happens to be from Trinidad, she said, "I'll have to make my own for you one time!" My version is low in added salt while incorporating a variety of vegetables and legumes in addition to the poultry. Don't be intimidated by the brine; it is a special technique that enhances the flavor of the chicken and keeps it extra juicy.

For the brine
½ cup honey

4 bay leaves

½ tablespoon cumin seed

½ tablespoon coriander seed

½ tablespoon whole black peppercorns

½ cup kosher salt

1 whole chicken (5 pounds), cut into 8 pieces

⅓ cup avocado oil

3 small yellow onions, minced

2 garlic cloves, minced

3 (1-inch) pieces fresh ginger

3 sprigs thyme

8 ounces pigeon peas, prepared according to the package directions

⅓ cup garlic chives

1 (13.5-ounce) can light coconut milk

1 teaspoon kosher salt

2 cups white basmati rice

Granny's Callaloo (page 114) or Jamaican-Style Callaloo (page 111), for serving

Make the brine: In a large pot, add the honey, bay leaves, cumin seed, coriander seed, peppercorns, and salt to 8 cups of water and stir until well combined. Add the chicken. Brine the chicken in the refrigerator for a minimum of 2 hours or ideally overnight. Remove the chicken from the brine and discard the liquid, pat dry, and set aside.

Heat a heavy-bottomed 10-quart pot over medium-high heat and add the oil and chicken. Brown the chicken for 4 to 5 minutes on each side, remove from the pot, and set aside.

Add the onion, garlic, and ginger to the pot and cook for 5 minutes.

Next, add the thyme, peas, chives, coconut milk, and salt and cook for 30 minutes. Finally, add the chicken and rice and 6 cups of water and cook for 20 minutes.

To serve, plate the pelau with a heaping spoonful of callaloo.

Vegetarian Alternative: For a vegetarian version, omit the chicken, reduce the amount of water to 5 cups, and cook for a total of 45 to 60 minutes.

RED WINE–BRAISED FRIED CHICKEN

(West and Central Africa)   Serves 4 to 6

WITH HOT HONEY

Fried chicken has long been a part of African American culture and cuisine. Slow food recipes have been handed down over generations and are steeped in history. You'll need to set aside 24 hours for this slow-braised method that makes the flavors sing. Don't despair—the vegetables from the brine get roasted and served alongside this culinary delight.

For the red wine brine

2 quarts red wine

2 bunches celery, diced

6 carrots, diced

3 large yellow onions, cut into quarters

2 whole garlic cloves

2 large bunches fresh thyme, plus more for garnish

3 star anise

2 tablespoons coriander seeds

4 large red beets, cut into quarters

Whole chicken, all parts separated

Substitution Tip: If you are not able to find palm oil, you can use 2 quarts of canola oil plus 2 quarts of avocado oil for frying.

For the dredge

6 large eggs

1 cup milk

8 cups flour

Kosher salt

Freshly ground black pepper

12 cups low-sodium bread crumbs

3 tablespoons paprika

2 quarts sustainably-sourced palm oil, for frying

2 quarts blended vegetable oil, for frying

For the spiced honey

1 cup honey

1 star anise, toasted

1 cinnamon stick

1 teaspoon whole black peppercorns, toasted

1 juniper berry

1 teaspoon ground allspice

Make the red wine brine: In a large pot, add the red wine, celery, carrots, onions, garlic, thyme, star anise, coriander, and beets and stir until well combined. Add the chicken. Brine the chicken in the refrigerator for 24 hours.

Preheat the oven to 275°F.

Recipe continues

MEAT

Place the chicken and brine in a large Dutch oven, cover with parchment paper then the lid, and bake for approximately 2½ hours, until thoroughly cooked. Remove from the oven and set aside until the liquid is cold, approximately 4 hours. Drain the chicken and pat dry, while reserving the vegetables.

Preheat the oven to 350°F.

Arrange the reserved vegetables on a sheet pan and bake for 25 minutes.

Meanwhile, make the dredge: In a medium bowl, whisk the eggs and milk together. In a large bowl, place the flour and season with salt and pepper. In another large bowl, place the bread crumbs and paprika. Coat the chicken in the flour mixture, then the egg/milk mixture, then the bread crumbs and set aside.

In a deep cast-iron skillet, heat the palm oil and blended vegetable oil until the temperature reaches 312°F. Fry the chicken until golden brown on both sides, around 5 minutes each, and season with salt while hot. (Note: The chicken is already fully cooked, so you are browning and reheating it during this process.)

Make the spiced honey: In a small saucepan over medium-low heat, add the honey, star anise, cinnamon stick, black peppercorns, juniper berry, and allspice and bring to a simmer. Cook for 5 to 7 minutes. Allow the honey to cool to room temperature and transfer to a heat-safe bowl.

To serve, place the fried chicken and roasted vegetables on a plate, drizzle honey on the chicken, and garnish with thyme leaves. Enjoy warm.

Frying was originally employed for chickens that had stopped laying eggs, so they were being "retired." Palm oil is the fat typically used throughout the African continent, especially in **Western Africa**, so if you can find sustainably produced palm oil, give it a try to fry this chicken.

COLLARD GREEN PATTY MELT

(East Africa)

Collard greens are the center of this patty melt. Cooked down enough to further break down the tender leaves and yield delicious pot likker. This is an open-faced patty that is stacked with vegetables, then the patty and cheese are finished off with a drizzle of pot likker.

2 tablespoons non-hydrogenated plant-based spread, plus more for cooking the burgers

2 bunches collard greens, leaves and stems separated, stems thinly chopped

2 yellow onions, thinly sliced

2 cups sliced dried shiitake mushrooms

2 tablespoons smoked paprika

¼ cup rice vinegar

1 tablespoon Tabasco

Kosher salt to taste

2¼ pounds grass-fed or grass-finished ground beef

Freshly ground black pepper

12 slices Gruyère or other Alpine cheese

1 loaf of local rye bread

In a large stockpot over medium-low heat, add the plant-based spread and collard stems and cook for 10 minutes.

Add the onions, cover, reduce to low heat, and cook for about 25 minutes, or until caramelized.

Julienne the collard leaves, add to the pot with 6 cups of water, cover, and cook for 15 minutes.

Add the mushrooms, smoked paprika, vinegar, and Tabasco, then season with salt. Drain the liquid, cool, and reserve in a jar to be used as gravy.

Make the patties: Season the beef with salt and pepper and form into 12 (3-ounce) patties.

Heat a cast-iron skillet over high heat, add plant-based spread and, in batches, hard sear the patties for 1 minute on each side, forming a crust.

Place 1 slice of cheese on each patty, cover the skillet with a lid, and cook for 4 to 5 minutes, until medium-rare. Continue until the patties are cooked.

Meanwhile, toast the bread.

To assemble, place ½ cup of collards on each slice of toast, then top with a patty. Drizzle gravy from the pot, known as pot likker, on each patty.

Chef Gerald told me that this patty melt celebrates foodways of the African diaspora by featuring sautéed collard greens, specifically inspired by **Kenya** and *sukuma wiki,* an East African dish that highlights sautéed collard greens, usually with meat. Hamburgers have become quintessentially American. This dish is a thought and an homage to two worlds' "sandwiched" together, producing an American hamburger

Ingredient Highlight: Collard greens are a great source of vitamins and fiber. If you are managing cardiometabolic conditions, fiber is beneficial for slowing down the absorption of sugar into the bloodstream, aiding in digestion and supporting healthy lipid levels.

BAHIAN-STYLE (Brazil)
CHICKEN WINGS
WITH SPICY TOMATOES AND COCONUT SAUCE

Bahian cuisine is influenced by indigenous flavors, African traditions, and Portuguese cuisine. These colorful wings are wrapped in a luscious spicy-tomato-and-coconut sauce that relies on the combination of vegetables, fruits, and spices to impart an incredible flavor. The recipe makes a large quantity of wings that are fit for a celebration.

For the chicken

5 pounds chicken wings

3 limes, cut into halves

3 lemons, cut into halves

1 cup white vinegar

2 tablespoons avocado oil

2 garlic cloves, minced

1 teaspoon kosher salt

¼ teaspoon freshly ground pepper

For the sauce

2 tablespoons olive oil

1 small white onion, diced

3 garlic cloves, minced

2 tablespoons minced fresh ginger

3 to 4 serrano peppers, seeded and finely diced

¼ cup finely diced red, yellow, or orange bell pepper

½ teaspoon smoked paprika

¼ teaspoon ground cumin

1 (14-ounce) can crushed tomatoes

1 (14-ounce) can coconut cream

¼ teaspoon kosher salt

Freshly ground black pepper to taste

¼ cup cilantro, chopped

Rice, for serving (optional)

Prepare the chicken: Begin by placing the chicken wings in a large bowl. Squeeze lime and lemon juice over the chicken and vigorously massage. Pour vinegar over the chicken mixture, and use the lemons and limes like scrub brushes to rub the wings. Discard the citrus and vinegar and pat the chicken dry. Preheat the oven to 400°F. Line a sheet pan with parchment paper.

In a large mixing bowl, combine the wings with the oil, garlic, salt, and pepper. Place the wings on the sheet pan. Bake for 40 to 45 minutes until the skin is browned and crispy.

Meanwhile, prepare the sauce: In a medium saucepan over medium heat, heat the oil. Add the onion, garlic, ginger, and peppers. Sauté for 6 to 7 minutes, stirring frequently, until the onions are translucent and soft. Add the paprika, cumin, tomatoes, coconut cream, and 1¾ cups of water, and simmer for 30 minutes, until the sauce has thickened and reduced. Season with salt and pepper.

To serve, arrange the chicken wings on a serving platter. Pour the sauce over the wings and top with the chopped cilantro. Serve as an appetizer or with rice as an entrée.

Ingredient Highlight: One tablespoon of paprika provides almost 20 percent of the recommended daily intake of vitamin A, a fat-soluble vitamin that is integral to eye health and immune function.

MEAT

As one of the most popular cuisines worldwide, Thai food is a beautiful flavor profile that is artfully layered. Geographically, Thailand is centrally located on mainland Southeast Asia. Its biodiversity and warm climate contribute to lush fertile lands. Thailand, previously known as Siam, was never colonized, although there were multiple attempts. In the 1930s, reforms transformed the country to a constitutional monarchy with one of the longest reigning kings in history.

Reaching as far back as the thirteenth century, influences from neighboring countries such as China and India inform Thai cuisine. Noodles and cooking in a wok are examples of food and culinary traditions that migrated to Thailand from China, while spices for Thai curries are influenced by Indian foodways. The neighboring Southeast Asian countries of Malaysia, Vietnam, and Indonesia have also made their imprint on Thai cuisine and vice versa.

Noodles are made in a variety of shapes and sizes and paired with distinct seasonings and sauces to make dishes like *pad kee moo*, a broad noodle drenched in saucy flavor, or *yum woon sen*, a glass noodle that can be made with most any protein of choice.

Regional variations are distinct. Curries and coconut milk–rich dishes are among the most well-known dishes from Thailand. Aromatic plants like onions, lemongrass, garlic, kaffir lime leaves, tamarinds, and ginger as well as herbs are incorporated into dishes. Sweet, sour, bitter, spicy, and salty are distinct flavors that surface in Thai cuisine and often come together in one dish. Rice, a staple, is used to make savory noodles as well as sweet sticky dishes.

PAD SEE EW *(Thailand)*

WITH CHICKEN

Chef Hong, who contributed this recipe, told me that in Thailand it's common to find krung poung, *a condiments rack, on the dining table so that you can season your noodles to your own taste. The condiments consist of fish sauce, pickled chili in vinegar, ground pepper, and sugar. Create your own* krung poung *for further customization of this savory protein-rich noodle dish.*

---

2 tablespoons avocado oil

1 teaspoon finely chopped garlic

2 large eggs

8 ounces boneless, skinless chicken breast or thigh, thinly sliced

8 ounces rice noodles, ½-inch-thick, soaked in warm water until completely softened

5 to 6 tablespoons pad see ew sauce

1 cup Chinese broccoli or kale leaves, cut into thin strips

Freshly ground white pepper

In a sauté pan or skillet, heat the oil over high heat. Once hot, work quickly and add the garlic and eggs. Use a spatula to break the eggs and sauté the garlic for about 1 minute or until the egg is almost cooked.

Add the chicken. Cook for 3 to 4 minutes or until the chicken is cooked.

Add the noodles and the sauce and cook for an additional 3 to 5 minutes. Add the Chinese broccoli and cook for an additional 5 minutes, stirring often.

To serve, transfer the noodles—being sure to include the eggs, chicken, and veggies—to a plate. Season with white pepper and enjoy.

Ingredient Highlight: Rice noodles, made from water and rice, are an excellent choice for those who follow gluten-free patterns of eating. They can be made with any rice (red, black, brown, or white), and the nutrient profiles will vary based on the rice used.

Tip: Looking for the most delicious pad see ew sauce? There is one available at ThaimeeLove.com, made by Chef Hong!

MEAT

LAAB MOO *(Thailand)*
CHIANG MAI
(CHIANG MAI–STYLE MINCED PORK)

Laab means "minced" in Thai, and so this dish is centered on minced meat. There are a number of varieties of laab in Thailand, each reflective of a regional style. This recipe is a classic from the north, specifically Chiang Mai, where Chef Hong grew up. In fact, this dish is a childhood favorite of Chef Hong's, beloved for its earthy flavor with a hint of the sea. Feel free to get creative with the garnishes and add vegetables that you enjoy.

1 pound ground pork

¼ pound pork liver, thinly sliced (optional)

1 tablespoon Thaimee Love laab chili, or more as needed

½ cup avocado oil

Dried Thai chilies to taste

4 garlic cloves, mashed and chopped

Nutrition Tip: Garlic has been linked to lowering blood pressure by modulating nitric oxide and hydrogen sulfide pathways in individuals with high blood pressure.

Purchasing Tip: The LOVE laab chili is available online at thaimeelove.com.

1 small shallot, thinly sliced

4 kaffir lime leaves, thinly sliced, or more as needed

2 stalks lemongrass (use 2 inches from the root), thinly sliced

1 tablespoon fish sauce, or more as needed, or kosher salt

1 sprig fresh cilantro, plus more for garnish

1 scallion, plus more for garnish

1 English cucumber, sliced, for serving

1 cup halved cherry tomatoes, for serving

Vegetables of your choice, for serving

In a large mixing bowl, mix the minced pork and pork liver (if using) with the chili seasoning. Set aside.

In a sauté pan, heat the avocado oil over medium-low heat. Add the chilies and fry for about 1 minute, or until they have darkened. Take them off the heat and rest them on a paper towel to drain the excess oil.

Add the garlic and shallots to the same sauté pan and cook for about 2 minutes, or until golden and fragrant. Be careful not to burn the garlic and shallots—the lower the heat the better. Once done, reserve half of the garlic and shallots for garnish. Leave the other half in the pan, turn up the heat, and add the minced pork mixture and cook for about 5 minutes, or until thoroughly cooked. Stir in half the kaffir lime leaves and half the lemongrass and cook, stirring, for another 2 minutes, until fragrant. Season with fish sauce or salt.

Transfer to a platter and garnish with the remaining kaffir lime leaves, remaining lemongrass, remaining shallots, crispy pork rinds, remaining fried garlic, fried Thai chilies, chopped cilantro, and scallions. Serve with cucumber, cherry tomatoes, and other vegetables of your choice.

Serving Tip: Traditionally, this dish is served with sticky rice, but jasmine rice will be fine. In central and northeastern Thailand, rice powder and lots of lime are used to season the dish.

FILIPINO (the Philippines)
PORK ADOBO

This Filipino-style adobo creates the perfect balance of salty, tangy, and peppery flavors and is the perfect dish to eat with rice. Be sure to leave enough time for the pork to soak up all of the seasonings. Once you make this dish, you'll want to make extra so that you have leftovers. Trust me, they are seriously delicious the next day!

2 pounds pork shoulder, cut into 1½-inch cubes

10 garlic cloves (5 cloves minced and 5 cloves sliced), plus additional for garnish

1 cup white vinegar

1 cup low-sodium soy sauce

2 teaspoons freshly ground black pepper

1 tablespoon sugar

1 small yellow onion, diced

⅛ teaspoon cayenne pepper (optional)

½ cup avocado oil

4 fresh bay leaves, or 2 dry

¼ cup full-fat coconut milk

In a large bowl, combine the pork shoulder, minced garlic, vinegar, soy sauce, black pepper, sugar, onion, and cayenne. Rub the pork until all the pieces are well-coated. Cover and place in the refrigerator to marinate for 2 to 12 hours.

In a cold large sauté pan, add ¼ cup of the avocado oil and the sliced garlic, and turn the heat to medium-low. Cook until lightly brown, then remove the garlic and set aside while reserving the oil.

Add the pork and marinade to the pan with 2 cups of water and the bay leaves. Bring to a boil over high heat, then reduce the heat to medium-low and simmer for 30 minutes. Remove from the heat and rest for 1 hour. Strain and save the liquid from the pan.

Add the remaining ¼ cup avocado oil to the same pan with the pork and cook until the meat browns. Add back the liquid, plus the coconut milk, bring to a boil, then simmer on low heat for 15 to 20 minutes.

To serve, transfer the adobo to a family-style serving platter and garnish with sliced garlic. Enjoy with a group of friends!

This is the unofficial national dish of **the Philippines**, according to Joel Javier. The word *adobo* is actually a cooking technique, which is why you'll find so many different varieties of this dish (and, of course, every culture considers their version to be the best!).

MEATBALLS  *(Scandinavia)*

Many traditional meatball recipes call for an equal ratio of ground pork to ground beef. If you don't eat pork, you can substitute ground chicken in its place. And if you don't eat beef, you can mix ground chicken and turkey, but you'll likely need to increase the seasoning to bring up the flavor. Be sure to pair this meatball with a low-added-sugar wild blueberry jam and boiled fingerling potatoes for an exquisite touch.

1 yellow onion, minced

1 pound ground pork

1 pound ground beef, 80% lean

½ teaspoon ground allspice or cloves

Freshly ground black pepper to taste

¼ teaspoon kosher salt

2 large eggs

2 cups whole wheat flour, for coating

4 tablespoons avocado oil

Fresh dill, for garnish

Wild blueberry jam, for serving

Boiled fingerling potatoes, for serving

In a large mixing bowl combine the onion, ground meat, allspice, black pepper, salt, and eggs. Knead together until all the ingredients are well-combined. With a clean wet hand, form golf ball-size meatballs and roll them in the whole wheat flour, then set aside.

Heat a large cast-iron skillet over medium-high heat and add the avocado oil. Add the meatballs and cook for 3 to 5 minutes on each side.

Garnish with fresh dill and serve with wild blueberry jam and boiled fingerling potatoes.

Ingredient Highlight: Blueberries are an excellent source of anthocyanins. Research has found that when consumed with an energy-dense meal, they have the ability to offset the impact of added sugars in people who have metabolic syndrome.

Ingredient Highlight: Cloves have a long history of being used as a medicinal spice. Current research is examining the positive health benefits associated with consuming cloves.

LAMB SOUVLAKI *(Greece)*
WITH TZATZIKI

Souvlaki is traditionally made on a skewer and can be prepared with a variety of animal proteins, including fish. This version is made in a cast-iron skillet for year-round enjoyment. The marinade is really what makes the dish, so allot enough time for your lamb to bathe in the flavorful goodness.

For the lamb

2 pounds lamb shoulder, cut into 1½-inch cubes

Juice of 2 lemons

Zest of 1 lemon

2 garlic cloves, smashed

½ cup coarsely chopped fresh sage

1 cup coarsely chopped fresh parsley

½ cup coarsely chopped fresh chives

¼ teaspoon kosher salt

¼ teaspoon freshly ground black pepper

¼ teaspoon ground cumin

2 tablespoons dried oregano

½ cup extra-virgin olive oil

For the tzatziki

8 ounces plain whole-milk Greek yogurt

2 Persian cucumbers, grated and strained

2 garlic cloves, grated

½ cup fresh mint leaves, thinly sliced

⅓ cup fresh dill, minced

Juice and zest of 1 large lemon

2 tablespoons extra-virgin olive oil

¼ teaspoon kosher salt, plus more for serving

¼ teaspoon freshly ground black pepper, plus more for serving

Make the lamb: In a large mixing bowl, place the lamb, lemon juice and zest, garlic, sage, parsley, chives, salt, pepper, cumin, oregano, and olive oil and massage together. Marinate for at least 30 minutes; the longer you allow the marinade to sit on the meat, the more flavorful it will be.

Remove the lamb from the marinade and place onto skewers. Heat a 12-inch cast-iron skillet over medium heat until smoking hot. Add the lamb skewers and sear for 3 to 5 minutes on each side, until golden brown.

Make the tzatziki: In a medium bowl, combine the yogurt, cucumbers, garlic, mint, dill, lemon juice and zest, olive oil, salt, and pepper and mix well. Season with additional salt and pepper to taste.

To serve, plate 4 to 5 lamb cubes with a spoonful of tzatziki.

Substitution Tip: If you are looking for a veggie option, swap the lamb skewers for a combination of seitan, mushrooms, and zucchini.

PERI PERI CHICKEN *(Portugal)*

This dish is a regional specialty from the town of Guia, in central Algarve. The flavors made their way to Portugal from Angola and Mozambique. Notably, this version is not intensely hot, but rather it has a more rounded heat that I would describe as layered. Every time I make it, I find myself standing over the sheet pan savoring every bite that has been left behind.

For the marinade

3 dried ancho chilies

3 tablespoons smoked paprika

1 tablespoon dried Aleppo pepper

4 garlic cloves

1 tablespoon ground coriander

¼ cup sherry vinegar

⅓ cup extra-virgin olive oil

½ teaspoon freshly ground black pepper

2 tablespoons fish sauce

1 (15-pound) chicken, butterflied and cleaned

Nutrition Tip: Fennel is a great source of fiber that helps to both slow the absorption of sugar into the bloodstream as well as support digestion.

For the herb sauce

½ cup finely chopped fresh cilantro with stems

½ cup finely chopped fresh dill

½ cup fresh parsley with stems, finely chopped

1 teaspoon ground coriander

Freshly ground black pepper

Juice and zest of 2 lemons

1 cup extra-virgin olive oil

For the salad

2 heads green leaf lettuce, washed and torn

1 fennel bulb with fronds, thinly sliced

Make the marinade: Place the chilies in a shallow dish and cover with water. Set aside for 15 to 20 minutes.

In a blender, place the rehydrated ancho chilies, paprika, Aleppo pepper, garlic, coriander, vinegar, oil, black pepper, fish sauce, and ¼ cup of water and blend until a smooth paste forms.

Line a sheet pan with parchment paper and place the chicken on the paper skin-side down. Generously cover the chicken in the marinade, massaging it into all the crevices, and leave for up to 24 hours in the refrigerator. Reserve some marinade for basting.

Preheat the oven to 400°F.

Place the chicken in the oven and bake for 30 minutes. Remove the chicken from the oven, brush the remaining marinade all over the chicken, flip the chicken, and cook covered in parchment paper for another 30 minutes.

Meanwhile, make the herb sauce: In a blender, place the cilantro, dill, parsley, coriander, pepper, lemon juice and zest, and oil and blend until smooth.

In a large mixing bowl, place the lettuce and fennel and dress with the herb sauce and toss. Set aside.

When the chicken is ready, remove it from the oven and let rest for at least 10 minutes, ideally 20 minutes, then carve.

To serve, enjoy the chicken with a heaping portion of salad and a generous drizzle of the herb sauce over everything.

Portugal is cradled between the Atlantic Ocean and the western side of Spain, and its cuisine has been heavily influenced by voyagers and colonizers' explorations along the coastline of western Africa, China, India, and Brazil as well as spice trade routes.

The coastal areas provide an abundance of seafood—often salted cod—and many dishes center on anchovies and crustaceans. Olive oils, herbs, spices, sausages of all kinds, and fresh breads to sop up soups feature heavily in Portuguese cuisine.

ABOUT
THE CHEFS

Chef Silvia

Silvia Barban was born and raised in Northern Italy from Venetian and Calabrian family.

From E. Maggia Stresa culinary school, Barban began to find her way in the kitchen of the maestro of Italian cuisine, Gualtiero Marchesi. She cooked modern and traditional dishes and learned more techniques for Giancarlo Perbellini. In 2012, she made the move to New York for the opening of Giovanni Rana Pastificio e Cucina. She was originally meant to be a part of a three-month consulting team but stayed on as sous chef, relishing the opportunity to work in Manhattan. After two years, Barban received an offer to become executive chef at Aita in Brooklyn and has directed the restaurant using fresh local produce to create traditional and modern Italian dishes from her native Italian heart. In 2016, she competed in season fourteen of Bravo's *Top Chef*. In 2016, she became the chef-owner of LaRina Pastificio e Vino in Fort Greene, Brooklyn.

Chef Vanessa

Vanessa Cantave is an executive chef, brand ambassador, culinary producer, and principal of NYC catering company Yum Yum. She has been featured on NBC's *The TODAY Show, Good Morning America,* A&E's *Homemade* series, the Cooking Channel, *The Wall Street Journal, NY Post, Essence* magazine, *Thrillist, Jet, Teen Vogue,* HuffPost, *Black Enterprise,* the *Better* show, *The Wendy Williams Show,* and *Ad Age.* She was named winner of Bravo's *Rocco's Dinner Party* hosted by Chef Rocco DiSpirito, where Master Chef Alain Sailhac described her winning dish as "the best short ribs I've had in my life!" *UPTOWN Magazine* described her food as "high-end flavor, but in a way you'd feel comfortable eating every day," and she famously taught ten New Yorkers how to prepare an easy and elegant brunch in *Essence* magazine. Her events and ambassadorship clients include Nike, L'Oréal, the NFL, Morgan Stanley, Google, Bacardi, Net-a-Porter, Cartier, Zillow, LVMH, Chrome Hearts, Timberland, Adidas, and Target. As a first generation Haitian American, she is passionate about doing her part to help rebuild Haiti following the devastating 2010 earthquake. Her work includes the Gout et Saveur Lakay Annual Food and Spirits festival aimed at driving tourism, generating awareness, and providing opportunities for aspiring young local chefs. Vanessa graduated as valedictorian from the French Culinary Institute in New York City. She completed her undergraduate studies at James Madison University and has a BA in political science, with a minor in French. Vanessa lives in Brooklyn and is mom to two boys, Christian (8) and Sebastien (3).

Chef Gerald

Born in St. Louis, Missouri, Chef Gerald fell in love with the process of cooking at a young age. Gerald worked his way up from dishwasher to chef de cuisine at the Westin St. Louis Cupples station. He would go on to work for Lou Rook at the iconic St. Louis restaurant Annie Gunn's. Gerald worked at Cielo located in the Four Seasons hotel under Chef Fabrizio Schneardi learning the "Italian hand" and traditions of that cuisine. Gerald's path then took him to Baltimore to work under Chef Michal Mina at the award-winning Wit and Wisdom. There he worked under Chef Clayton Miller, giving form to an upscale mid-Atlantic tavern. Gerald was tapped to open PBG at the Four Season's Orlando, where he was able to hone his skills with live fire and a rotisserie. Gerald made his way to Marco Island to take the helm of Ario. He built the restaurant's dry ages program and offers diners a global nomadic lens through food. Gerald was chosen to be a contestant on *Top Chef* season 14, filmed in Charleston. Gerald also hosted his own dinner at the eponymous James Beard House in July 2017. Gerald opened the ornate Tesoro in 2018, giving way to an elevated experience both figuratively and literally as the restaurant overlooks the Gulf of Mexico from five stories high. Modern Mediterranean is the cuisine. Gerald also runs 10k Alley, a gastro pub housed in a 10,000-square-foot gaming and entertainment space. Gerald is currently opening Knife and Spoon at the Ritz Carlton Orlando Grande Lakes, for which he is the first black male chef to receive a Michelin star. Gerald is a frequent featured talent at some of the country's most sought-after culinary festivals including Aspen, Atlanta, Charleston, and Pebble Beach. Gerald was also featured at the James Beard House in 2019 with fellow *Top Chef* alums for Silvia Barban's inaugural dinner. Chef Gerald is also a level two certified WSET Sommelier.

Chef Priyanka

Priyanka Naik is a self-taught Indian vegan chef, Food Network champion, Quibi *Dishmantled* winner, TV personality, author of *The Modern Tiffin,* and columnist of "EcoKitchen" for *The Washington Post*! An avid traveler who's been to nearly forty countries, her globally inspired original recipes, with a focus on sustainability, have been featured on her blog *Chef Priyanka,* and on *TODAY Table*—an NBC Peacock TV show that she co-hosts—and are incorporated into her regular speaking appearances. She has garnered attention from and been featured on *The Kelly Clarkson Show, Forbes, Glamour,* three times *The TODAY Show*-featured chef in Studio 1A, *Bon Appétit* miniseries, CNN, *GQ,* The Beet, Well+Good, Medium, and more. She has partnered with hundreds of brands globally, including JUST Egg, Planet Oat, Coca-Cola, Amazon, Walmart, and Spotify for brand campaigns. Priyanka is a first-generation Indian American raised on Staten Island, New York, and has two older sisters. Her Indian heritage is very important to her cooking style and lifestyle, so much so that she even learned her native language of Kannada before English and weaves in Indian elements throughout all of her original vegan cooking. She attributes her devotion to her Indian roots and passion for Indian food to her loving and supportive parents.

Chef Hong

Originally from Chiang Mai, Thailand, Hong Thaimee is a chef, entrepreneur, and philanthropist who has served as a global ambassador for Thai cuisine and culture for nearly a decade. She first won critical acclaim for her restaurant, Ngam, in New York's East Village, where she introduced her style of modern Thai comfort food. In 2015, Hong published her first cookbook, *True Thai* (Rizzoli), displaying her vivacious personality, skill, and passion for the unique flavors of her homeland. Now one of the most visible faces of Thai food in the US, Hong has been invited to cook at prestigious venues around the world, including New York's Metropolitan Museum of Art, the James Beard House, and for numerous five-star hotel brands. She has appeared on TV in the US and across Southeast Asia, including on Food Network's *Iron Chef America*, in a major TV campaign for Air Asia, and as a judge on a prominent Thai cooking series. Hong currently serves on City Harvest's Food Council and is a Global Chef Ambassador for the AIDS charity (RED). Hong's latest venture, Thaimee Love, is a culinary company and brand that includes a pop-up restaurant in New York's West Village, virtual cooking classes, and a line of Thai products and meal kits. Additionally, Hong is collaborating with Heermance Farm in the Hudson Valley to grow Thai ingredients and source the freshest local meat, seafood, and produce for her restaurant. A portion of the proceeds from Thaimee Love benefits City Harvest and ROAR, an organization raising funds for hospitality professionals impacted by the COVID-19 pandemic.

Chef Joel

Chef Joel Javier was born in Quezon City, Philippines, and raised in Jersey City, New Jersey. Surrounded by family who loved to cook and loved to eat even more, Javier's relationship with food had been fostered around the dinner table. Javier graduated from Johnson and Wales University with an associate's degree in culinary arts in 2001 and a bachelor's degree in food service management in 2003. Joel Javier has been a chef in New York City for the past seventeen years. He creates refined and thoughtful dining experiences through his evolving cuisine. Inspired by his travels in Asia and Europe, and his Filipino roots, along with his experience from working alongside Michelin-starred chefs, Javier's personalized menus cover a wide array of preferences, with New American–Filipino food as his flagship cuisine. With a focus on local and seasonal ingredients, he offers a unique and flavorful menu, including dietary restrictions such as vegan and gluten-free options.

Javier, together with his wife, Rachel, owns and runs Flip Eats, where they create custom meals and experiences, including but not limited to private dinners, catering, pop-ups, weekly meals, and special events.

Chef Elizabeth

Elizabeth Falkner was born in San Francisco, grew up in Los Angeles, and worked her way up in San Francisco's top kitchens before opening her first restaurant, Citizen Cake, in 1997. A decade later, she opened four more restaurants in San Francisco and New York. Today, she does recipe development and consults on numerous products and brands. She is an inspiring public speaker and has cooked and spoken all over the United States and in Japan, Europe, Mexico, Canada, and China. Falkner's style of cuisine is globally inspired, and she cooks both savory and sweet, traditional and modern. She is an advocate for people and chefs to think more like athletes and "stay fit to cook." She played league soccer for twenty-eight years and has studied Jungshin and Iadō—both are forms of sword fighting fitness and martial arts. She also practices yoga on a regular basis, does CrossFit, Pilates, half marathons and the New York City Marathon in 2016, cycling, and tennis. Cooking competitions are a favorite "sport" for Chef Elizabeth. She has competed and judged for the last fifteen years on many of the television cooking competition programs for Food Network, Cooking Channel, Bravo, and NBC, as well as made appearances on many other shows. She was nominated for the James Beard Award for Outstanding Pastry Chef (2005). A graduate of the San Francisco Art Institute with a BFA in film, Falkner produces films with food themes, and she is also working on a series of food-inspired interactive installations and a memoir.

ACKNOWLEDGMENTS

This cookbook was truly born from the love of food and culture and has the imprints of chefs who helped me craft this love letter to the globe.

To Chef Silvia Barban, you are my favorite person to share a kitchen with; your enjoyment of flavor helped each of these recipes glow. You taught me how to gently use salt and not to shy away from the artful incorporation of sugar and fat into meals. For this my palate is eternally grateful. I thank you for your friendship and collaboration.

To Chef Vanessa, you provided guidance on transforming classic tastes. Chef Gerald, you are a culinary master who brought me to tears. Thank you for loving food and sharing it with me. Chef Joel, you bring integrity and joy to the kitchen—I can hear your laugh when I think of you. Chef Hong, your spices transport us all across the ocean. Thank you for sharing your unique flavors with me. Chef Falkner, thank you for your contributions. And Chef Priyanka, it's a pleasure and honor to know you as well as to have your contributions.

And my family, I am because of you. My husband, Vinz, and children, Parker and Anaïs, are always open to my kitchen takeovers and exotic foods that come into the home. To my mother, Jacqui, and late mother, Virginia, and her wife, Ilene, and my "Papi" Gerdés and his wife, Florienne—so much of me comes from each of you.

My friends who inspired me, tasted and shared feedback, laughed with me and cried, too—I thank each of you and am grateful for the community we have built together. My patients and students for helping me to be a forever learner, thank you. My colleagues who took my calls and created levity in moments of challenge—thank you.

My team: Josanne, you always have my back and keep me moving forward. Rebecca, your work ethic is unmatched and your dedication to sharing my voice is deeply moving. Karina, your kind and gentle manner in the eye of the storm is much appreciated. Thank you.

The dietetic interns, Jason Leeve, Rebekah Jarvis, and Laine Strobel, RD, who quite literally rolled with it—thank you for your thoughts, contributions, conversations, and nutrition research.

Christine, your eye is unmatched. Thank you for curating the most amazing photography team—Monica, you, and Debbie—not only did the studio smell amazing, but also together you made each recipe shine. Gerri, prop mistress extraordinaire, your love of color and creative pieces provided the most interesting vessels and exquisite backdrops for the recipes. Rae, thanks for your assistance. Alex, you made my skin glow and the food pop! Kvarøy Artic, thank you for the donation of the most beautiful salmon.

To the folx at Goop, Kiki in particular, thank you for giving me a platform to share my passion, love, and appreciation for history, tradition, food, and nutrition. Donna, my editor, thank you for providing major guidance and helping me to shape the story and get this cookbook into print.

And to you, the readers, thank you for your curiosity and willingness to expand your palates. Happy eating and reading!

NOTES

12 **Where I live in New York**
"Type 2 Diabetes," NYC Health, https://www1.nyc.gov/site/doh/
health/health-topics/diabetes.page (accessed June 19, 2021).

12 **According to the Centers for Disease Control**
"Heart Disease Facts," Centers for Disease Control and
Prevention,
https://www.cdc.gov/heartdisease/facts.htm#:~:text=Heart
%20Disease%20in%20the%20United%20States&text=
One%20person%20dies%20every%2036,1%20in%20every
%204%20deaths.&text=Heart%20disease%20costs%20
the%20United,year%20from%202014%20to%202015
(accessed February 7, 2022).

12 **Health outcomes are impacted by where someone lives**
"Social Determinants of Health," World Health Organization,
https://www.who.int/health-topics/social-determinants-of
-health#tab=tab_1.

13 **There is a significant link**
Megan E. Harrison, Mark L. Norris, Nicole Obeid, Maeghan
Fu, Hannah Weinstangel, and Margaret Sampson,
"Systematic Review of the Effects of Family Meal Frequency
on Psychosocial Outcomes in Youth." *Canadian Family
Physician Medecin de famille canadien* 61, no. 2 (2015),
https://www.ncbi.nlm.nih.gov/pmc/articles/PMC4325878.

27 **For your meats**
Cynthia A. Daley, Amber Abbott, Patrick S. Doyle, Glenn
A. Nader, and Stephanie Larson, "A Review of Fatty Acid
Profiles and Antioxidant Content in Grass-Fed and Grain-Fed
Beef," *Nutrition Journal* 9, no. 1 (2010), https://doi
.org/10.1186/1475-2891-9-10.

27 **Pasture-raised eggs and poultry**
H. D. Karsten, P. H. Patterson, R. Stout, and G. Crews,
"Vitamins A, E and Fatty Acid Composition of the Eggs of
Caged Hens and Pastured Hens," *Renewable Agriculture and
Food Systems* 25, no. 1 (2010): 45–54, https://doi.org/10.1017/
s1742170509990214.

27 **Pasture-raised eggs and poultry**
Julia Kühn, Alexandra Schutkowski, Holger Kluge, Frank
Hirche, and Gabriele I. Stangl, "Free-Range Farming:
A Natural Alternative to Produce Vitamin D-Enriched Eggs,"
Nutrition 30, no. 4 (2014): 481–84, https://doi.org/10.1016/j
.nut.2013.10.002.

27 **Similar to beef**
Brad Heins, "Grass-Fed Cows Produce Healthier Milk,"
University of Minnesota Extension, https://extension.umn
.edu/pasture-based-dairy/grass-fed-cows-produce-healthier
-milk (accessed July 14, 2021).

30 **Most major global health agencies**
"Healthy Diet," World Health Organization, https://www.who
.int/news-room/fact-sheets/detail/healthy-diet (accessed
March 8, 2022).

34 **Refined Oils**
Amy C. Brown, *Understanding Food: Principles and
Preparation* (Belmont: Wadsworth Cengage Learning, 2011).

34 **Refined Oils**
Carmen Dobarganes and Gloria Márquez-Ruiz, "Possible
Adverse Effects of Frying with Vegetable Oils," *British
Journal of Nutrition* 113, no. S2 (2015), https://doi
.org/10.1017/s000 7114514002347.

34 **Refined Oils**
"Ask the Expert: Concerns about Canola Oil," The Nutrition
Source, Harvard School of Public Health, last updated
December 21, 2018, https://www.hsph.harvard.edu/
nutritionsource/2015/04/13/ask-the-expert-concerns-about
-canola-oil.

34 **Refined Oils**
"Healthful Oils: The Canola Controversy," Today's Dietitian,
https://www.todaysdietitian.com/newarchives/1018p12.shtml.

34 **Refined Oils**
H. Su, R. Liu, M. Chang, J. Huang, X. Wang, "Dietary Linoleic
Acid Intake and Blood Inflammatory Markers: A Systematic
Review and Meta-Analysis of Randomized Controlled Trials,"
Food & Function 8, no. 9 (2017), https://pubmed.ncbi.nlm.nih
.gov/28752873.

35 **The World Health Organization**
"WHO Guideline: Sugar Consumption Recommendation,"
World Health Organization, https://www.who.int/news/
item/04-03-2015-who-calls-on-countries-to-reduce-sugars
-intake-among-adults-and-children (accessed July 14, 2021).

35 **And the American Heart Association**
"Added Sugars," American Heart Association, last modified
November 2, 2021, https://www.heart.org/en/healthy-living/
healthy-eating/eat-smart/sugar/added-sugars.

35 **The WHO recommends**
"WHO Guideline: Sugar Consumption Recommendation," World Health Organization, https://www.who.int/news/ item/04-03-2015-who-calls-on-countries-to-reduce-sugars -intake-among-adults-and-children#:~:text=A%20new%20 WHO%20guideline%20recommends,would%20provide%20 additional%20health%20benefits (accessed February 21, 2022).

35 **Herbs and spices**
T. Alan Jiang, "Health Benefits of Culinary Herbs and Spices," *Journal of AOAC INTERNATIONAL* 102, no. 2 (2019): 395–411, https://doi.org/10.5740/jaoacint.18-0418.

36 **Dashi powder is a combination**
Qian-Qian Mao, Xiao-Yu Xu, Shi-Yu Cao, Ren-You Gan, Harold Corke, Trust Beta, and Hua-Bin Li, "Bioactive Compounds and Bioactivities of Ginger (*Zingiber officinale* Roscoe)," *Foods* 8, no. 6 (2019) 185, https://www.ncbi.nlm.nih.gov/pmc/articles/ PMC6616534.

38 **Recommended modifications**
A. Chatterjee, S. B. Harris, L. A. Leiter, D. H. Fitchett, H. Teoh, O. K. Bhattacharyya, "Managing Cardiometabolic Risk in Primary Care: Summary of the 2011 Consensus Statement," *Canadian Family Physician Medecin de famille canadien* 58, no. 4 (2012), https://pubmed.ncbi.nlm.nih.gov/22611605.

42 **Einkorn flour**
S. Bo, M. Seletto, A. Choc, V. Ponzo, A. Lezo, A. Demagistris, A. Evangelista, G. Ciccone, M. Bertolino, M. Cassader, R. Gambino, "The Acute Impact of the Intake of Four Types of Bread on Satiety and Blood Concentrations of Glucose, Insulin, Free Fatty Acids, Triglyceride and Acylated Ghrelin. A Randomized Controlled Cross-over Trial," *Food Research International* 92 (2017), https://pubmed.ncbi.nlm.nih .gov/28290296.

45 **If you are being mindful**
Jo Ann Carson, Alice H. Lichtenstein, Cheryl A. M. Anderson, Lawrence J. Appel, Penny M. Kris-Etherton, Katie A. Meyer, Kristina Petersen, Tamar Polonsky, and Linda Van Horn, "Dietary Cholesterol and Cardiovascular Risk: A Science Advisory from the American Heart Association," *Circulation* 141, no. 3 (2020), https://www.ahajournals.org/doi/10.1161/ CIR.0000000000000743.

45 **Cayenne peppers**
Angela M. Chapa-Oliver and Laura Mejía-Teniente, "Capsaicin: From Plants to a Cancer-Suppressing Agent," *Molecules* 21, no. 8 (August 2016), https://www.ncbi.nlm.nih.gov/pmc/articles/ PMC6274000.

47 **Cassava flour has**
Nancy F. Sheard, et al., "Dietary Carbohydrate (Amount and Type) in the Prevention and Management of Diabetes: A statement by the American Diabetes Association," *Diabetes Care* 27, no. 9 (2004), https://care.diabetesjournals.org/ content/27/9/2266.long (accessed June 23, 2021).

47 **Cassava flour has**
Thomas M. Wolever, et al., "Prediction of the Relative Blood Glucose Response of Mixed Meals Using the White Bread Glycemic Index," *Diabetes Care* 8, no. 5 (1985), https://care .diabetesjournals.org/content/8/5/418.short.

48 **Chives—along with other allium vegetables**
Yahya Asemani, Nasrindokht Zamani, Maryam Bayat, and Zahra Amirghofran, "Allium Vegetables for Possible Future of Cancer Treatment," *Phytotherapy Research* 33, no. 12 (2019): 3019–39, https://doi.org/10.1002/ptr.6490.

53 **Asparagus is a great source**
B. Kulczyński, J. Kobus-Cisowska, D. Kmiecik, A. Gramza-Michałowska, D. Golczak, J. Korczak, "Antiradical Capacity and Polyphenol Composition of Asparagus Spears Varieties Cultivated under Different Sunlight Conditions," *Acta scientiarum polonorum Technologia alimentaria*, https:// pubmed.ncbi.nlm.nih.gov/28071026.

57 **If you are managing blood sugars**
Nancy F. Sheard et al., "Dietary Carbohydrate (Amount and Type) in the Prevention and Management of Diabetes: A statement by the American Diabetes Association," *Diabetes Care* 27, no. 9 (2004), https://care.diabetesjournals.org/ content/27/9/2266.long (accessed April 27, 2022).

57 **If you are managing blood sugars**
Thomas M. Wolever, et al., "Prediction of the Relative Blood Glucose Response of Mixed Meals Using the White Bread Glycemic Index," *Diabetes Care* 8, no. 5 (1985), https://care .diabetesjournals.org/content/8/5/418.short.

NOTES

57 Coconut milk is a great plant-based source
Fabian M. Dayrit, "The Properties of Lauric Acid and Their
Significance in Coconut Oil," *Journal of the American Oil
Chemists' Society*, 92, 1–15 (2015), https://doi.org/10.1007/
s11746-014-2562-7.

59 Whole wheat flour is less refined
Sebastian Åberg, Jim Mann, Silke Neumann, Alastair B. Ross,
and Andrew N. Reynolds, "Whole-Grain Processing and
Glycemic Control in Type 2 Diabetes: A Randomized Crossover
Trial," *Diabetes Care* 43, no. 8 (2020): 1717–23, https://doi
.org/10.2337/dc20-0263.

59 Whole wheat flour is less refined
Giuseppe Della Pepa, Claudia Vetrani, Marilena Vitale, and
Gabriele Riccardi, "Wholegrain Intake and Risk of Type 2
Diabetes: Evidence from Epidemiological and Intervention
Studies," *Diabetes Care* 27, no. 9 (204): 2266–71, https://doi
.org/10.3390/nu10091288.

60 If supporting healthy blood lipid levels
Jo Ann Carson, Alice H. Lichtenstein, Cheryl A. M. Anderson,
Lawrence J. Appel, Penny M. Kris-Etherton, Katie A.
Meyer, Kristina Petersen, Tamar Polonsky, and Linda Van
Horn, "Dietary Cholesterol and Cardiovascular Risk: A
Science Advisory from the American Heart Association,"
Circulation 141, no. 3 (2020), https://doi.org/10.1161/
cir.0000000000000743.

63 Black pepper is used
Sahdeo Prasad, Amit K. Tyagi, and Bharat B. Aggarwal, "Recent
Developments in Delivery, Bioavailability, Absorption and
Metabolism of Curcumin: The Golden Pigment from Golden
Spice," *Cancer Research and Treatment* 46, no. 1 (2014): 2–18,
https://doi.org/10.4143/crt.2014.46.1.2.

72 Oats are packed with fiber
Chunye Chen, Yuan Zeng, Jing Xu, Hongting Zheng, Jun Liu,
Rong Fan, Wenyi Zhu, et al., "Therapeutic Effects of Soluble
Dietary Fiber Consumption on Type 2 Diabetes Mellitus,"
Experimental and Therapeutic Medicine 12, no. 2 (2016):
1232–42, https://doi.org/10.3892/etm.2016.3377.

72 Oats are packed with fiber
Marc P. McRae, "Dietary Fiber Intake and Type 2 Diabetes
Mellitus: An Umbrella Review of Meta-Analyses," *Journal of
Chiropractic Medicine* 17, no. 1 (2018): 44–53, https://doi
.org/10.1016/j.jcm.2017.11.002.

73 Sourdough bread is made with
Siew Wen Lau, Ann Qi Chong, Nyuk Ling Chin, Rosnita A.
Talib, and Roseliza Kadir Basha, "Sourdough Microbiome
Comparison and Benefits," *Microorganisms* 9,
no. 7 (2021): 1355, https://doi.org/10.3390/
microorganisms9071355.

75 Fiber alert
Chunye Chen, Yuan Zeng, Jing Xu, Hongting Zheng, Jun Liu,
Rong Fan, Wenyi Zhu, et al., "Therapeutic Effects of Soluble
Dietary Fiber Consumption on Type 2 Diabetes Mellitus,"
Experimental and Therapeutic Medicine 12, no. 2 (2016):
1232–42, https://doi.org/10.3892/etm.2016.3377.

75 Fiber alert
Marc P. McRae, "Dietary Fiber Intake and Type 2 Diabetes
Mellitus: An Umbrella Review of Meta-Analyses," *Journal of
Chiropractic Medicine* 17, no. 1 (2018): 44–53, https://doi
.org/10.1016/j.jcm.2017.11.002.

76 If you are thinking about your blood sugars
Sebastian Åberg, Jim Mann, Silke Neumann, Alastair B. Ross,
and Andrew N. Reynolds, "Whole-Grain Processing and
Glycemic Control in Type 2 Diabetes: A Randomized Crossover
Trial," *Diabetes Care* 43, no. 8 (2020): 1717–23, https://doi
.org/10.2337/dc20-0263.

76 If you are thinking about your blood sugars
Giuseppe Della Pepa, Claudia Vetrani, Marilena Vitale, and
Gabriele Riccardi, "Wholegrain Intake and Risk of Type 2
Diabetes: Evidence from Epidemiological and Intervention
Studies," *Nutrients* 10, no. 9 (2018): 1288, https://doi
.org/10.3390/nu10091288.

76 If you are thinking about your blood sugars
Otilia Bobiş, Daniel S. Dezmirean, and Adela Ramona Moise,
"Honey and Diabetes: The Importance of Natural Simple Sugars
in Diet for Preventing and Treating Different Type of Diabetes,"
Oxidative Medicine and Cellular Longevity 2018 (2018): 1–12,
https://doi.org/10.1155/2018/4757893.

78 Figs are a nutrient-rich fruit
Mark Dreher, "Whole Fruits and Fruit Fiber Emerging
Health Effects," *Nutrients* 10, no. 12 (2018): 1833, https://doi.
org/10.3390/nu10121833.

83 Parsley is a powerhouse herb
James J. DiNicolantonio, Jaikrit Bhutani, and James H. O'Keefe,
"The Health Benefits of Vitamin K," *Open Heart*, 2, no. 1 (2015),
https://www.ncbi.nlm.nih.gov/pmc/articles/PMC4600246.

83 Parsley is a powerhouse herb
"Fooddata Central Search Results," FoodData Central, U.S.
Department of Agriculture, Agricultural Research Service,
https://fdc.nal.usda.gov/fdc-app.html#/food-details/170416/
nutrients (accessed April 27, 2022).

85 This curry powder is
Susan J. Hewlings, and Douglas S. Kalman, "Curcumin: A
Review of Its Effects on Human Health," *Foods* 6, no. 10 (2017),
https://www.ncbi.nlm.nih.gov/pmc/articles/PMC5664031.

NOTES

86 **Saffron, the most expensive spice**
"Why Is Saffron So Expensive?" Encyclopædia Britannica,
https://www.britannica.com/story/why-is-saffron-so
-expensive.

86 **Saffron, the most expensive spice**
H. A. Hausenblas, D. Saha, P. J. Dubyak, and S. D. Anton,
"Saffron (*Crocus sativus L.*) and Major Depressive Disorder:
A Meta-Analysis of Randomized Clinical Trials," *Journal of
Integrative Medicine* 11, no. 6 (2013): 377–83, https://pubmed
.ncbi.nlm.nih.gov/24299602.

89 **Berbere is a spice**
Sunil K. Panchal, Edward Bliss, Lindsay Brown, "Capsaicin in
Metabolic Syndrome," *Nutrients* 10, no. 5 (2018): 630, https://
pubmed.ncbi.nlm.nih.gov/29772784.

91 **Allspice, an aromatic spice**
Lei Zhang and Bal L. Lokeshwar, "Medicinal Properties of the
Jamaican Pepper Plant Pimenta dioica and Allspice," Current
Drug Targets 13, no. 1(2012): 1900–06, https://www.ncbi.nlm
.nih.gov/pmc/articles/PMC3891794.

95 **This recipe is packed with fiber**
Chunye Chen, Yuan Zeng, Jing Xu, Hongting Zheng, Jun Liu,
Rong Fan, Wenyi Zhu, et al., "Therapeutic Effects of Soluble
Dietary Fiber Consumption on Type 2 Diabetes Mellitus,"
Experimental and Therapeutic Medicine 12, no. 2 (2016):
1232–42, https://doi.org/10.3892/etm.2016.3377.

95 and 107 **If you are not able to find**
Chunye Chen, Yuan Zeng, Jing Xu, Hongting Zheng, Jun Liu,
Rong Fan, Wenyi Zhu, et al., "Therapeutic Effects of Soluble
Dietary Fiber Consumption on Type 2 Diabetes Mellitus,"
Experimental and Therapeutic Medicine 12, no. 2 (2016):
1232–42, https://doi.org/10.3892/etm.2016.3377.

96 **If you are managing diabetes**
Yuanming Zhang, Dingyun You, Nanjia Lu, Donghui Duan,
Xiaoqi Feng, Thomas Astell-Burt, Pan Zhu, Liyuan Han, Shiwei
Duan, and Zuquan Zou, "Potatoes Consumption and Risk of
Type 2 Diabetes: A Meta-Analysis," *Iranian Journal of Public
Health* 47, no. 11 (2018): 1627–35, https://www.ncbi.nlm.nih.gov/
pmc/articles/PMC6294859.

97 **Olive oil is a great source**
Carla Assaf-Balut, Nuria García de la Torre, Alejandra Durán,
Manuel Fuentes, Elena Bordiú, Laura del Valle, Cristina Familiar,
et al., "A Mediterranean Diet with Additional Extra Virgin
Olive Oil and Pistachios Reduces the Incidence of Gestational
Diabetes Mellitus (GDM): A Randomized Controlled Trial: The
St. Carlos GDM Prevention Study," PLOS ONE, October 19,
2017, https://doi.org/10.1371/journal.pone.0185873.

97 **Olive oil is a great source**
Javier Delgado-Lista, Pablo Perez-Martinez, Antonio Garcia-
Rios, Juan F. Alcala-Diaz, Ana I. Perez-Caballero, Francisco
Gomez-Delgado, Francisco Fuentes, et al., "Coronary Diet
Intervention with Olive Oil and Cardiovascular Prevention
Study (the CORDIOPREV Study): Rationale, Methods, and
Baseline Characteristics," *American Heart Journal* 177 (2016):
42–50, https://doi.org/10.1016/j.ahj.2016.04.011.

103 **Togarashi, also known as**
N. Rajapakse, S. K. Kim, "Nutritional and Digestive Health
Benefits of Seaweed," *Advances in Food and Nutrition
Research* 64 (2011) 17–28, https://pubmed.ncbi.nlm.nih
.gov/22054935.

105 **Swap frozen sweet corn**
Yuanming Zhang, Dingyun You, Nanjia Lu, Donghui Duan,
Xiaoqi Feng, Thomas Astell-Burt, Pan Zhu, Liyuan Han, Shiwei
Duan, and Zuquan Zou, "Potatoes Consumption and Risk of
Type 2 Diabetes: A Meta-Analysis," *Iranian Journal of Public
Health* 47, no. 11 (2018): 1627–35, https://www.ncbi.nlm.nih.gov/
pmc/articles/PMC6294859.

111 **Callaloo refers to the leafy dark greens**
Xiaojie Yuan, Xiaochun Li, Zhaohua Ji, Jing Xiao, Lei Zhang,
Weilu Zhang, Haixiao Su, Kanakaraju Kaliannan, Yong Long,
and Zhongjun Shao, "Effects of Vitamin C Supplementation
on Blood Pressure and Hypertension Control in Response
to Ambient Temperature Changes in Patients with Essential
Hypertension," *Clinical and Experimental Hypertension* 41,
no. 5 (2018): 414–21, https://doi.org/10.1080/10641963.2018.1
501056.

111 **Callaloo refers to the leafy dark greens**
Tommaso Filippini, Federica Violi, Roberto D'Amico, and Marco
Vinceti, "The Effect of Potassium Supplementation on Blood
Pressure in Hypertensive Subjects: A Systematic Review and
Meta-Analysis," *International Journal of Cardiology* 230
(2017): 127–35, https://doi.org/10.1016/j.ijcard.2016.12.048.

112 **Dashi powder is a combination**
W. M. Marx, L. Teleni, A. L. McCarthy, L. Vitetta, D.
McKavanagh, D. Thomson, E. Isenring, "Ginger (*Zingiber
officinale*) and Chemotherapy-Induced Nausea and Vomiting:
A Systematic Literature Review," *Nutrition Reviews* 71, no. 4
(2013): 245–54, https://pubmed.ncbi.nlm.nih.gov/23550785.

114 **Avocado oil is an excellent substitute**
Marcos Flores, Carolina Saravia, Claudia E. Vergara, Felipe
Avila, Hugo Valdés, and Jaime Ortiz-Viedma, "Avocado Oil:
Characteristics, Properties, and Applications," *Molecules*
24, no. 11 (2019): 2172, https://doi.org/10.3390/
molecules24112172.

NOTES

116 **Cumin and cumin seeds**
Qing Liu, Xiao Meng, Ya Li, Cai-Ning Zhao, Guo-Yi Tang, and Hua-Bin Li, "Antibacterial and Antifungal Activities of Spices," *International Journal of Molecular Sciences* 18, no. 6 (2017): 1283, https://www.ncbi.nlm.nih.gov/pmc/articles/PMC5486105.

118 **Anchovies are a rich source**
JoAnn E. Manson, Nancy R. Cook, I-Min Lee, William Christen, Shari S. Bassuk, Samia Mora, Heike Gibson, et al., "Marine N–3 Fatty Acids and Prevention of Cardiovascular Disease and Cancer," *New England Journal of Medicine* 380, no. 1 (2019): 23–32, https://doi.org/10.1056/nejmoa1811403.

119 **Betalain, a water-soluble pigment**
Chunye Chen, Yuan Zeng, Jing Xu, Hongting Zheng, Jun Liu, Rong Fan, Wenyi Zhu, et al., "Therapeutic Effects of Soluble Dietary Fiber Consumption on Type 2 Diabetes Mellitus," *Experimental and Therapeutic Medicine* 12, no. 2 (2016): 1232–42, https://doi.org/10.3892/etm.2016.3377.

119 **Betalain, a water-soluble pigment**
Marc P. McRae, "Dietary Fiber Intake and Type 2 Diabetes Mellitus: An Umbrella Review of Meta-Analyses," *Journal of Chiropractic Medicine* 17, no. 1 (2018): 44–53, https://doi.org/10.1016/j.jcm.2017.11.002.

119 **Betalain, a water-soluble pigment**
Yuan, Xiaojie Yuan, Xiaochun Li, Zhaohua Ji, Jing Xiao, Lei Zhang, Weilu Zhang, Haixiao Su, Kanakaraju Kaliannan, Yong Long, and Zhongjun Shao, "Effects of Vitamin C Supplementation on Blood Pressure and Hypertension Control in Response to Ambient Temperature Changes in Patients with Essential Hypertension," *Clinical and Experimental Hypertension* 41, no. 5 (2018): 414–21, https://doi.org/10.1080/10641963.2018.1501056.

119 **Betalain, a water-soluble pigment**
Tommaso Filippini, Federica Violi, Roberto D'Amico, and Marco Vinceti, "The Effect of Potassium Supplementation on Blood Pressure in Hypertensive Subjects: A Systematic Review and Meta-Analysis," *International Journal of Cardiology* 230 (2017): 127–35, https://doi.org/10.1016/j.ijcard.2016.12.048.

123 **Sunny mushrooms**
"Mushrooms," The Nutrition Source, Harvard School of Public Health, last updated March 2, 2022, https://www.hsph.harvard.edu/nutritionsource/food-features/mushrooms.

128 **Black sesame seeds**
"Office of Dietary Supplements: Copper," National Institutes of Health Office of Dietary Supplements, U.S. Department of Health and Human Services, https://ods.od.nih.gov/factsheets/Copper-HealthProfessional.

124 **This recipe is packed with fiber**
Marc P. McRae, "Dietary Fiber Intake and Type 2 Diabetes Mellitus: An Umbrella Review of Meta-Analyses," *Journal of Chiropractic Medicine* 17, no. 1 (2018): 44–53, https://doi.org/10.1016/j.jcm.2017.11.002.

124 **Sumac is a flowering shrub**
A. H. Alghadir, S. A. Gabr, "Efficacy of Rhus Coriaria (Sumac) Juice in Reducing Muscle Pain During Aerobic Exercise," *Physiology International* 103, no. 2 (2016): 231–242, https://pubmed.ncbi.nlm.nih.gov/28639865.

128 **Black sesame seeds**
"Fooddata Central Search Results," FoodData Central, U.S. Department of Agriculture, Agricultural Research Service, https://fdc.nal.usda.gov/fdc-app.html#/food-details/703474/nutrients (accessed April 27, 2022).

129 **When using canned**
Andrea Grillo, Lucia Salvi, Paolo Coruzzi, Paolo Salvi, and Gianfranco Parati, "Sodium Intake and Hypertension," *Nutrients* 11, no. 9 (2019): 1970, https://doi.org/10.3390/nu11091970.

130 **Duck eggs are an excellent source**
"Fooddata Central Search Results," FoodData Central, U.S. Department of Agriculture, Agricultural Research Service, https://fdc.nal.usda.gov/fdc-app.html#/food-details/172189/nutrients (accessed March 10, 2022).

132 **Eggs are a great source**
Heqian Kuang, Fang Yang, Yan Zhang, Tiannan Wang, and Guoxun Chen, "The Impact of Egg Nutrient Composition and Its Consumption on Cholesterol Homeostasis," *Cholesterol* 2018 (2018): 1–22, https://doi.org/10.1155/2018/6303810.

132 **Eggs are a great source**
P. Schnohr, , O. Ø. Thomsen, P. Riis Hansen, G. Boberg-Ans, H. Lawaetz, and T. Weeke, "Egg Consumption and High-Density-Lipoprotein Cholesterol," *Journal of Internal Medicine* 235, no. 3 (1994): 249–51, https://doi.org/10.1111/j.1365-2796.1994.tb01068.x.

140 **Native to the Andes region**
Chunye Chen, Yuan Zeng, Jing Xu, Hongting Zheng, Jun Liu, Rong Fan, Wenyi Zhu, et al., "Therapeutic Effects of Soluble Dietary Fiber Consumption on Type 2 Diabetes Mellitus," *Experimental and Therapeutic Medicine* 12, no. 2 (2016): 1232–42, https://doi.org/10.3892/etm.2016.3377.

140 **Native to the Andes region**
Marc P. McRae, "Dietary Fiber Intake and Type 2 Diabetes Mellitus: An Umbrella Review of Meta-Analyses," *Journal of Chiropractic Medicine* 17, no. 1 (2018): 44–53, https://doi.org/10.1016/j.jcm.2017.11.002.

NOTES

145 **If you are being mindful**
Kate S. Driscoll, Amanda Appathurai, Markandeya Jois, and Jessica E. Radcliffe, "Effects of Herbs and Spices on Blood Pressure," *Journal of Hypertension* 37, no. 4 (2019): 671–79, https://doi.org/10.1097/hjh.0000000000001952.

150 **Edible flowers enhance**
E. Lara-Cortés, P. Osorio-Díaz, A. ;Jiménez-Aparicio, S. Bautista-Baños. "[Nutritional Content, Functional Properties and Conservation of Edible Flowers. Review]," *Archivos Latinoamericanos de Nutricion* 63, no. 3 (2013): 197–208, https://pubmed.ncbi.nlm.nih.gov/25362819.

152 **Artichoke is a good source**
M. Ben Salem, H. Affes, K. Ksouda, R. Dhouibi, Z. Sahnoun, S. Hammami, K. M. Zeghal KM, "Pharmacological Studies of Artichoke Leaf Extract and Their Health Benefits," *Plant Foods for Human Nutrition* 70, no. 4 (2015): 441– 53, https://pubmed.ncbi.nlm.nih.gov/26310198.

159 **Botanically, okra is a fruit**
Arezoo Moradi, Moahammad Javad Tarrahi, Sara Ghasempour, Mohammadreza Shafiepour, Cain C. Clark, and Sayyed Morteza Safavi, "The Effect of Okra (*Abelmoschus esculentus*) on Lipid Profiles and Glycemic Indices in Type 2 Diabetic Adults: Randomized Double Blinded Trials," *Phytotherapy Research* 34, no. 12 (2020): 3325–32, https://doi.org/10.1002/ptr.6782.

161 **Choclo, a large kernel**
Kari Hatlestad, "The Social and Cultural Origins of Peruvian Food" (master's thesis, Portland State University, 2017), https://doi.org/10.15760/honors.360.

171 **Making your own seasoning**
Andrea Grillo, Lucia Salvi, Paolo Coruzzi, Paolo Salvi, and Gianfranco Parati, "Sodium Intake and Hypertension," *Nutrients* 11, no. 9 (2019): 1970, https://doi.org/10.3390/nu11091970.

175 **Fresh dill**
Mohammad Taghi Goodarzi, Iraj Khodadadi, Heidar Tavilani, and Ebrahim Abbasi Oshaghi, "The Role of *Anethum graveolens* L. (Dill) in the Management of Diabetes," *Journal of Tropical Medicine*, 2016, https://www.ncbi.nlm.nih.gov/pmc/articles/PMC5088306.

175 **Salmon is an excellent source**
Chisa Matsumoto, Ayhan Yoruk, Lu Wang, J. Michael Gaziano, and Howard D. Sesso, "Fish and Omega-3 Fatty Acid Consumption and Risk of Hypertension," *Journal of Hypertension* 37, no. 6 (2019): 1223–29, https://doi.org/10.1097/hjh.0000000000002062.

175 **Salmon is an excellent source**
Ingrid V. Hagen, Anita Helland, Marianne Bratlie, Karl A. Brokstad, Grethe Rosenlund, Harald Sveier, Gunnar Mellgren, and Oddrun A. Gudbrandsen, "High Intake of Fatty Fish, but Not of Lean Fish, Affects Serum Concentrations of Tag and HDL-Cholesterol in Healthy, Normal-Weight Adults: A Randomised Trial," *British Journal of Nutrition* 116, no. 4 (2016): 648–57, https://doi.org/10.1017/s0007114516002555.

175 **Tarragon in large quantities**
Miriam Méndez-del Villar, Ana M. Puebla-Pérez, María J. Sánchez-Peña, Luis J. González-Ortiz, Esperanza Martínez-Abundis, and Manuel González-Ortiz, "Effect of *Artemisia dracunculus* Administration on Glycemic Control, Insulin Sensitivity, and Insulin Secretion in Patients with Impaired Glucose Tolerance," *Journal of Medicinal Food* 19, no. 5 (2016): 481–85, https://doi.org/10.1089

177 **Red snapper is a great source**
Chisa Matsumoto, Ayhan Yoruk, Lu Wang, J. Michael Gaziano, and Howard D. Sesso, "Fish and Omega-3 Fatty Acid Consumption and Risk of Hypertension," *Journal of Hypertension* 37, no. 6 (2019): 1223–29, https://doi.org/10.1097/hjh.0000000000002062.

177 **Red snapper is a great source**
Ingrid V. Hagen, Anita Helland, Marianne Bratlie, Karl A. Brokstad, Grethe Rosenlund, Harald Sveier, Gunnar Mellgren, and Oddrun A. Gudbrandsen, "High Intake of Fatty Fish, but Not of Lean Fish, Affects Serum Concentrations of Tag and HDL-Cholesterol in Healthy, Normal-Weight Adults: A Randomised Trial," *British Journal of Nutrition* 116, no. 4 (2016): 648–57, https://doi.org/10.1017/s0007114516002555.

183 **Most of the sodium we consume**
Niels Albert Graudal, Thorbjorn Hubeck-Graudal, and Gesche Jurgens, "Effects of Low Sodium Diet versus High Sodium Diet on Blood Pressure, Renin, Aldosterone, Catecholamines, Cholesterol, and Triglyceride," *Cochrane Database of Systematic Reviews*, 2011, https://doi.org/10.1002/14651858.cd004022.pub3.

183 **Most of the sodium we consume**
Andrea Grillo, Lucia Salvi, Paolo Coruzzi, Paolo Salvi, and Gianfranco Parati, "Sodium Intake and Hypertension," *Nutrients* 11, no. 9 (2019): 1970, https://doi.org/10.3390/nu11091970.

187 **If you are not able to find**
Marc P. McRae, "Dietary Fiber Intake and Type 2 Diabetes Mellitus: An Umbrella Review of Meta-Analyses," *Journal of Chiropractic Medicine* 17, no. 1 (2018): 44–53, https://doi.org/10.1016/j.jcm.2017.11.002.

NOTES

190 Heat a cast-iron skillet over high heat

Ankit Goyal, Vivek Sharma, Neelam Upadhyay, Sandeep Gill, and Manvesh Sihag, "Flax and Flaxseed Oil: An Ancient Medicine & Modern Functional Food," *Journal of Food Science and Technology* 51, no. 9 (2014): 1633–53, https://www.ncbi.nlm.nih.gov/pmc/articles/PMC4152533.

191 One tablespoon of paprika

"Fooddata Central Search Results," FoodData Central, U.S. Department of Agriculture, Agricultural Research Service, https://fdc.nal.usda.gov/fdc-app.html#/food-details/171329/nutrients (accessed June 24, 2021).

196 Garlic has been linked

Karin Ried, "Garlic Lowers Blood Pressure in Hypertensive Subjects, Improves Arterial Stiffness and Gut Microbiota: A Review and Meta-Analysis," *Experimental and Therapeutic Medicine*, 2019, https://doi.org/10.3892/etm.2019.8374.

200 Cloves have a long history

Ratheesh Mohan, Svenia Jose, Johannah Mulakkal, Darla Karpinsky-Semper, Andrew G. Swick, and I. M. Krishnakumar, "Water-Soluble Polyphenol-Rich Clove Extract Lowers Pre- and Post-Prandial Blood Glucose Levels in Healthy and Prediabetic Volunteers: An Open Label Pilot Study," *BMC Complementary and Alternative Medicine* 19, no. 1 (2019), https://doi.org/10.1186/s12906-019-2507-7.

200 Cloves have a long history

Renny Reji Mammen, Johannah Natinga Mulakal, Ratheesh Mohanan, Balu Maliakel, and Krishnakumar Illathu Madhavamenon, "Clove Bud Polyphenols Alleviate Alterations in Inflammation and Oxidative Stress Markers Associated with Binge Drinking: A Randomized Double-Blinded Placebo-Controlled Crossover Study," *Journal of Medicinal Food* 21, no. 11 (2018): 1188–96, https://doi.org/10.1089/jmf.2017.4177.

Functi

200 Blueberries are an excellent source

Peter J. Curtis, Lindsey Berends, Vera van der Velpen, Amy Jennings, Laura Haag, Preeti Chandra, Colin D. Kay, Eric B. Rimm, and Aedín Cassidy, "Blueberry Anthocyanin Intake Attenuates the Postprandial Cardiometabolic Effect of an Energy-Dense Food Challenge: Results from a Double Blind, Randomized Controlled Trial in Metabolic Syndrome Participants," *Clinical Nutrition* 41, no. 1 (2022): 165–76, https://doi.org/10.1016/j.clnu.2021.11.030.

202 Fennel is a great source

Chunye Chen, Yuan Zeng, Jing Xu, Hongting Zheng, Jun Liu, Rong Fan, Wenyi Zhu, et al., "Therapeutic Effects of Soluble Dietary Fiber Consumption on Type 2 Diabetes Mellitus," *Experimental and Therapeutic Medicine* 12, no. 2 (2016): 1232–42, https://doi.org/10.3892/etm.2016.3377.

202 Fennel is a great source

Marc P. McRae, "Dietary Fiber Intake and Type 2 Diabetes Mellitus: An Umbrella Review of Meta-Analyses," *Journal of Chiropractic Medicine* 17, no. 1 (2018): 44–53, https://doi.org/10.1016/j.jcm.2017.11.002.

INDEX

INDEX

MAYA FELLER, MS, RD, CDN, founder
of Brooklyn-based Maya Feller Nutrition, is
a nationally recognized registered dietitian
nutritionist. She received her master's of science
in clinical nutrition from New York University.
Maya shares her approachable, culturally fluent,
real food–based solutions through regular
speaking engagements, writing for local and
national publications, and as a nutrition expert
on *Good Morning America* and more.